trotman

CW00369726

Getting Into

Oxford &
Cambridge

Sarah Alakija

10th edition

Getting into Oxford & Cambridge

This tenth edition published in 2007 by Trotman, an imprint of Crimson Publishing, Richmond, Surrey TW9 2ND

© Trotman 1987, 1989, 1991, 1994, 1996, 1999, 2001, 2003, 2005, 2007.
Reprinted 2005, 2006, 2007.

Editorial and Publishing Team
Author Sarah Alakija
Editorial Mina Patria, Publishing Director; Jo Jacomb, Editorial Manager; Jessica Spencer, Development Editor; Ian Turner, Production Editor
Production John O'Toole, Operations Manager;
Jaqui Palmer, Art Director; Tom Hulatt, Junior Designer;
Lorcan Mulligan, Production Controller
Advertising Sarah Talbot, Advertising Manager (020 8334 1617)

British Library Cataloguing in Publication Data
A catalogue record for this book is available from the British Library

ISBN 978 1 84455 142 2

Typeset by Ian Turner

Printed and bound in Great Britain by Creative Print & Design (Wales) Ltd

Contents

For up-to-date information on Oxford and
Cambridge go to www.mpw.co.uk/getintooxb

ACKNOWLEDGEMENTS

The tenth edition of *Getting into Oxford & Cambridge* was updated and revised by Sarah Alakija of MPW. She would like to thank Janet Graham and Sarah Hannaford of the Cambridge Admissions Office for their input and invaluable help. She would also like to thank James Burnett and Mario Di Clemente of MPW, as well as all the students who provided feedback from their Oxford and Cambridge interviews.

INTRODUCTION

This book should be read in conjunction with the universities' own prospectuses and the individual college prospectuses. Its main purpose is not to repeat the factual information that you will find in the prospectuses, but rather to provide sometimes quite subjective advice that will help you make the most of your application and to avoid some of the common pitfalls. The less you already know about Oxbridge, its courses and colleges, its admissions procedures and what to expect at interview, the more useful you will find this publication.

The author of this book is an Oxford graduate, with over 10 years' experience of helping sixth formers make applications to Oxford and Cambridge and is on hand if you wish to speak to her informally.

The book begins by giving a general flavour of the two universities before moving on to the considerations which should be uppermost in your mind when choosing your subject, university and college. It then deals with the selection procedure – making the most of your personal statement, the written work that you submit, the tests that you are given at interview and the interview itself. Finally, this latest edition brings readers up to date with the most recent available statistical information on subject entries at different colleges, and updates the popular sections on interview technique and sample questions.

'I don't know about any of the colleges', *'I don't know what the courses involve in detail'* and *'I don't trust myself not to freeze if I can't answer a technical question at interview'* are all common worries. If you're worrying about any of these, this book is for you. One of the intentions in writing it is to dispel the myth that it is only the Oxbridge 'inner circle' who can apply to Oxbridge. That is not what the universities think and it should not be what you think. With a little groundwork, there is no reason why you cannot be as competitive as any applicant with your academic credentials. Good luck!

1

OVERVIEW

WHAT ARE OXFORD AND CAMBRIDGE LIKE?

Memorable. Unforgettable. Drop into your local library and you'll find a selection of books containing reminiscences of Oxford or Cambridge, not to mention the inevitable crop of guide books to the cities. Turn to the fiction section and you'll discover that many novelists have used these cities and their universities as settings for their work. Waugh's *Brideshead Revisited*, CP Snow's *The Masters*, Max Beerbohm's *Zuleika Dobson* and Stephen Fry's *The Liar* are some of the most well known. More recently the dramatisation of Sharpe's *Porterhouse Blue* and the *Inspector Morse* series have brought Cambridge and Oxford respectively on to the television.

Few graduates of Oxford or Cambridge will deny that their university experience has in many ways affected their whole lives, and most will need little prompting to express vivid memories of those three or four important years. These educational institutions arouse passions and affection. Everybody seems to have his or her own ideas about what Oxford and Cambridge are like.

By any standards they are large universities. Cambridge has a student body of about 17,000, of whom some 11,500 are undergraduates and Oxford has a student body of approximately 18,000, of whom also around 11,500 are undergraduates. Both are ancient religious foundations: the first Oxford college was established in 1249, some 35 years before the first college at Cambridge. Both are famed for their research and teaching. Both offer a wide range of courses. If they sound rather similar institutions, it is not surprising... they are. Few at either Oxford or Cambridge may agree though, as pride in each university's own character is strong. Competition between them lies deeper than the Boat Race, but the rivalry is friendly and continues as a tradition.

Nevertheless, we talk about Oxford and Cambridge in the same breath. It has even been necessary to invent a collective word to describe them.

Oxbridge has been accepted into the language and can be found in most English dictionaries. We see the two universities in the same light and in the same league – and so, of course, do they. What binds them together in everybody's minds, in a unique alliance, is a combination of history and standards. Both reach levels of excellence that are respected throughout the world and thus they attract teaching staff of a very high calibre. The standards survived both the great university expansion of the 1960s and 1970s and the financial restraints of the 1980s. Both are equally determined not to allow the tuition fees reforms of the late 1990s to dilute their reputations for academic excellence for students from all walks of life.

That is not to say that there aren't other good, indeed great, universities in Britain. There are, and they should be considered seriously in your application.

Is it just standards that set Oxford and Cambridge apart? Some people believe that their exclusivity stems from the way they operate and the way they have developed their collegiate and tutorial/supervision system. It's a system that other universities have tried to emulate but not entirely successfully. It is a unique model that lies at the very centre of the character of Oxbridge.

To an outsider the system must seem a little bizarre. No modern planner would design a university with colleges dotted all over town. The collegiate system may appear untidy but it works well, and for the undergraduates who make their way to Oxford or Cambridge it provides an excellent teaching base.

Oxford and Cambridge, though large universities, are really federations of relatively small colleges. Admitting undergraduates, Oxford has 30 colleges and seven permanent private halls, while Cambridge has 29 colleges. They are as follows:

OXFORD COLLEGES

Balliol College	Oriel College
Brasenose College	Pembroke College
Christ Church	The Queen's College
Corpus Christi College	St Anne's College
Exeter College	St Catherine's College
Harris Manchester College	St Edmund Hall
Hertford College	St Hilda's College
Jesus College	St Hugh's College
Keble College	St John's College
Lady Margaret Hall	St Peter's College
Lincoln College	Somerville College
Magdalen College	Trinity College
Mansfield College	University College
Merton College	Wadham College
New College	Worcester College

OXFORD PERMANENT PRIVATE HALLS

Blackfriars	St Benet's Hall
Campion Hall	St Stephen's House
Greyfriars	Wycliffe Hall
Regent's Park College	

CAMBRIDGE COLLEGES

Christ's College	Homerton College
Churchill College	Hughes Hall
Clare College	Jesus College
Corpus Christi College	King's College
Downing College	Lucy Cavendish College
Emmanuel College	Magdalene College
Fitzwilliam College	New Hall
Girton College	Newnham College
Gonville & Caius College	Pembroke College

Peterhouse
Queens' College
Robinson College
St Catharine's College
St Edmund's College
St John's College

Selwyn College
Sidney Sussex College
Trinity College
Trinity Hall
Wolfson College

The universities have a shared responsibility with the colleges for the tuition of students but their roles are very different – they are complementary rather than in competition, with each providing different facilities. For further information on each of the colleges see Chapter 4.

THE ROLE OF THE UNIVERSITY

EXAMINATIONS

The university determines the courses that are offered and the content of the syllabuses. It conducts examinations and confers degrees. So, whatever college you join, the course you follow will be essentially the same. The university provides a wide range of facilities such as laboratories (including language laboratories), central lecture halls, libraries, museums, a computer centre and much more besides.

FACULTIES

Both universities are structured on a faculty system and within a particular faculty students from all colleges covering the same course will meet for lectures, classes, seminars, practicals and laboratory work. The overall importance of the educational role of the university in a student's academic career will depend very much on the course being read. The university's role is much greater for science than for arts students. For the former, there are generally more lectures to attend – sometimes as many as ten a week – as well as two or three weekly practical laboratory sessions. Although not all lectures and practicals are strictly compulsory, they form the basis on which the course is structured. Arts students, on the other hand, find their academic life is usually more college-based; for them, lectures are fewer and more optional. A tutor in an arts subject might, for instance, recommend that a session in the library could be more beneficial than an hour in the lecture hall.

SPORTS AND SOCIETIES

The role of the university is not just confined to academic life, however. It provides the forum for many activities — sports, politics, drama, journalism, music and so on. The Boat Race and Varsity matches and the occasional furore triggered by an Oxford Union debate, or the more recent demonstrations about tuition fees, show the life of the universities breaking into the wider world.

Because the universities can draw on the abilities of people from all the colleges, standards can be high, providing an excellent testing ground for talent. The cricket and rugby teams of both universities, for example, meet first-class opposition and countless past members of the debating and drama societies of Oxford and Cambridge are now household names.

Most sporting and leisure activities are duplicated by the colleges and this gives wider opportunities to more students. College activities — music, drama, politics and so on — tend to be more relaxed and take their style from the college and its members. Recruitment to these societies is usually by word of mouth, an announcement on the notice board or a knock on the door. Recruitment to university societies, however, is by means of a fair held at the beginning of each academic year at which societies advertise their activities and tout for new members from the fresh intake of students.

THE ROLE OF THE COLLEGE

The universities are large. At times, they may appear a little formidable. The colleges, on the other hand, are usually small, friendly communities of between 200 and 1,000 students, with a warm atmosphere and an environment which caters for the needs of the individual. Each Oxford or Cambridge college is an independent, self-governing, self-contained unit. It makes its own decisions, selects the students it wants and provides the facilities and approach to study it thinks are best. The colleges are proud of their independence and individuality, their resources and their records of success.

WHAT IS THE TEACHING LIKE?

The success of the teaching at Cambridge and Oxford is widely accepted as being due to the *tutorial system* as it is known at Oxford, or *supervisions* as they are called at Cambridge. Despite the different names, they are essentially the same and *tutorial* is used below to describe both.

You are generally responsible for your own learning and you will find the materials you need at lectures and in the faculty libraries at your disposal. Each week you will have been set a piece of work which you will have been expected to research yourself. You will then meet with your subject tutor around once a week or once a fortnight to discuss in depth the tasks which you have been set. The tutorials generally consist of between one and four students only, so you have the opportunity to review your work and raise questions with leading academics in your subject on a very individual basis. Depending on your subject, the tutorial will consist of frank and critical discussion of your work. You will be encouraged to debate the issues you have researched as well as defend your opinions and criticise others where necessary. Your powers of independent thought and analysis will be tested to the hilt as the philosophy behind the tutorial is to encourage you to test out new ideas, to see things from other points of view, to construct a valid argument and to give and receive constructive criticism.

Your tutorial will generally last about one hour and may take place in your chosen college with a specialist from that college, but where there is no fellow to cover that subject you may find that you have tutorials in other colleges. This is where the collegiate system can take advantage of its role within the university to ensure that you receive the best teaching from experts in your chosen subject.

To benefit from the above system you do need to be prepared to motivate yourself, as you are the only person really responsible for your learning. Obviously there are people to help and advise you but the ultimate decision is yours and it is this freedom which so many undergraduates cherish. There will be nobody there to hold your hand and make you go to tutorials and lectures so you need to be self-motivated and truly interested in your subject. If you are, and you can work well under pressure, you will succeed.

THE OXBRIDGE ATMOSPHERE

Both Oxford and Cambridge offer a stimulating environment for the individual and a haven for the eccentric.

Historically, Oxford may have had something of a reputation for being the university for the arts and Cambridge for the sciences. But these reputations are now largely misleading and the ratio of arts to science students in both universities is about even. Cambridge graduates are never slow to point out that while it was the university for Newton and Darwin, it also produced Byron, Milton and Wordsworth. Oxford developed penicillin and produced Boyle's Law as well as Shelley and WH Auden. Today, Oxford has no reason to take second place to Cambridge in the study of the sciences. It is possible that the one-time bias of the two universities has had an effect on the individual character and atmosphere, but if it has, it is largely indiscernible.

The atmosphere at Oxford and Cambridge is competitive. Students expect to succeed in whatever they are doing. In acting, journalism, sport, music, politics or their academic work, many push themselves to the limit or beyond. Stamina is an important quality. There are three Oxbridge terms in a year and each is only eight weeks long. A great deal of work and life is thus crammed into a short space of time. The pace can be hectic and the intellectual and social intensity exhausting. Some college libraries stay open all night – an indication of the pressure that can build up for students.

GETTING A PLACE

Some of the admission processes may appear bewildering at first sight – *Why do I have to make an application directly to the university as well as through UCAS? Should my personal statement be the same for both? How do I choose a college? Do I need a PhD (or DPhil!) in Statistics so that I can analyse past entry patterns by course and by college? Do I have to worry about grouping (Oxford)? Why can't I choose my own second and third choice colleges? Should I make an open application? What does it mean if I am pooled?*

Don't worry about these questions for the moment. They will be dealt with later. For now, stay calm and remember three things:

- It's easy to rule out a college if it does not offer your subject. Otherwise, the choice of college is in general probably less important than the choice of course and university, and should not be agonised over if you are uncertain.
- Strategic planning on the basis of historical college-by-college entry statistics is risky – we present the entry statistics in Chapter 4 in order to give you a feel for student numbers, not as a way of enabling you to predict which college will be easier to get into (there's broadly no such thing).
- You are not expected to be an expert on the colleges before you start applying, or to know everything about the college that you have selected once you have chosen it.

Interviews vary, as do interviewers. Some tutors are more shrewd than others and better judges of ability and character. All interviews, however, are likely to be searching and to last about half an hour. In Chapter 6, there is some advice on what to expect in your interview.

Stories about eccentric interviewers abound, but many are much elaborated. You may have heard the story about the young man who came into the interview room to find the tutor hidden behind a copy of *The Times*. 'Surprise me,' snapped the tutor from behind the paper, whereupon the student set light to the newspaper and, so the story goes, immediately gained entrance to Oxbridge. Although this story is almost certainly false, a surprise that goes down well with the interviewer, whether the interviewer is eccentric or not, can be a key determinant in getting you noticed.

The selection procedure at both universities has evolved in recent years, partly to cut down on administration and partly to encourage applications from the state sector. Applicants are now assessed on the basis of their academic background and (where appropriate) their predicted grades at A level, their personal statements and references, on the written work that they submit prior to interview and at interview, and on their performance at the interview itself. For applicants who have already taken their A level exams, an offer that is made will be unconditional. For those yet to take A levels, conditional offers vary from AAA to AAB (and very occasionally ABB).

AS LEVEL CHOICES

Some students are unsure as to which subjects are acceptable when applying for an Oxbridge place. Both universities have stated that they normally expect applicants to be studying for four AS levels in the first year of sixth form.

In their respective prospectuses, the universities list their preferred A level subjects for each degree course. Some subjects require specific A level subjects as an essential entry requirement; others state certain subjects as being useful. Cambridge has published a list of A level subjects which it states are advisable to take for general entry and another of those A level subjects which it does not feel prepare a student sufficiently for undergraduate study. The latter list is reproduced below. Cambridge recommends that prospective students should generally be studying only *one* of the subjects in the list below and the remaining subjects should be of the more traditional academic type.

- Accounting
- Art and Design (check Architecture)
- Business Studies
- Communication Studies
- Dance
- Design and Technology (check Engineering)
- Drama/Theatre Studies
- Film Studies
- Health and Social Care
- Home Economics
- Information and Communication Technology
- Leisure Studies
- Media Studies

■ Music Technology
■ Performance Studies
■ Performing Arts
■ Photography
■ Physical Education
■ Sports Studies
■ Travel and Tourism.

The subjects should cover a range of skills. For example, the universities are looking for scientists who can also show linguistic skills and for arts students who are also numerate and able to apply rules of logic.

The basic rule when choosing your subjects if you are a prospective Oxbridge applicant (or an applicant for any other university, to be honest) is to choose subjects which ensure you use a variety of skills. All undergraduates, regardless of their course, need to be able to write in clear and succinct prose, to be able to think in a logical fashion and to know how to use evidence to back up their arguments. Try to pick subjects which show that you have all these skills.

ADVANCED EXTENSION AWARDS

Advanced Extension Awards (AEAs) are based on A level subject criteria and provide opportunities for students to show logical and critical thinking skills and a greater depth of understanding than required at A level.

Cambridge sometimes use AEAs as part of their offers. Details are given below:

■ Christ's – may include an AEA as part of a conditional offer in any subject. You should contact the college for further information.
■ Emmanuel – may ask Medicine, Veterinary Medicine and Natural Sciences applicants taking only two science/mathematics subjects for an AEA in one of the science subjects that they are studying.
■ Gonville and Caius – asks Computer Science applicants for AEA in Maths.
■ Trinity – asks Engineering applicants not taking Further Maths at A level for a Merit in AEA in Maths.

NOT YOUR TYPICAL OXBRIDGE STUDENT?

There are many preconceptions about the type of student who is attracted to and accepted at Oxford and Cambridge – white, middle-class, privately educated, straight-A student etc etc. To some extent, it could be said that myths like these are based on fact somewhere along the line and although the above description may well have encompassed the majority of Oxbridge undergraduates a number of years ago, both the universities are doing a great deal to change this and have had success.

You don't have to be a genius to get into Oxford or Cambridge. If you have good grades in a range of GCSEs or the equivalent it could be worth your while applying. The universities are committed to admitting the most able students irrespective of background and are actively seeking to encourage applications from groups that are currently under-represented.

STATE SCHOOL V PUBLIC SCHOOL

Over the last few years, the Oxbridge application process has come under very close scrutiny following Oxford's rejection of a state school student with five A grades at A level who went on to win a scholarship to Harvard. More recently, Oxford has been much criticised for rejecting deaf student Anastasia Fedotova who achieved six A grades at A level only five years after arriving in the UK. It is claimed that Trinity College, Cambridge, sneered at the aspirations of Essex schoolgirl Tracy Playle when they asked whether she understood the 'funny squiggles' of a line of Greek in a poem.

After each rejection was reported, politicians, education-alists and the press were in uproar denouncing the unfairness of the application procedure. Even the then Home Secretary called for the process to be made clearer to state school applicants. So should you be put off from applying if you are from a state school? The answer really has to be 'No', as the two universities are making great efforts to make the interview process fairer to all applicants.

It should always be remembered, however, that only one in four of the students who are interviewed can be accepted as there are quite simply not enough places for all of them. Most of the students who apply and are subsequently interviewed are of above-average academic ability and go on to get three A grades at A level. In fact 91% of the students admitted to Cambridge in 2003 gained those grades or higher. The point is that excellent students have to be rejected wherever they may go to school. At both Oxford and Cambridge the most recent statistics show that 59% of offers made are to state school applicants and 41% are to those from the independent sector.

Both universities now have training for interviewers in order to combat discrimination of any kind including against state school applicants. At Cambridge, interviewers have to attend equal opportunities training as well as practising their techniques on sixth form volunteers. Sixth form tutors are encouraged to visit the universities in order to gain a clearer idea of the admissions process and the reality of interviews. Schools and applicants are now sent a copy of guidelines for interviews as well. It is hoped that these measures will help to dispel some of the myths which surround the process and will allow schools to prepare students from a more informed perspective.

Have these changes placed applicants from the independent and maintained sectors on a more equal footing? A comparison of 2005 entry statistics by type of school provides an intriguing discussion point for those interested in the sociology of education.

	Oxford		Cambridge	
	Applying	Accepted	Applying	Accepted
Maintained	5,809	1,490	6,624	1,643
Independent	4,388	1,410	4,195	1,360
Other/overseas	2,299	314	2,881	432
Total	**12,496**	**3,214**	**13,700**	**3,435**

The independent schools still have the slight lead in success rates once an application has been made, but more striking is the small number of maintained school applications in the first place (bearing in mind their overall share of the post-16 market). Part of the explanation may lie in typical responses heard while researching this book from those in the state sector:

It's elitist.
It's snobbish.
I'd be made to feel inferior.
They're all Hooray Henrys.
Everyone would be high fliers, real academics, and I'm not ultra-clever.
It would be too expensive.

The Oxford Access Scheme targets inner city schools in particular and helps teachers through the application processes. Open days and conferences are set up in order to ensure that potential students are fully aware of what Oxford has to offer.

The Cambridge Special Access Scheme's main function is to focus on the problems faced by those who do not have a history of applying to university. The scheme allows these students to have their cases stated more fully at application. You are eligible if very few people from your school go on to higher education and your family has little tradition of studying for a degree. You may also use the scheme if your education has been disrupted through health or personal problems.

The Cambridge University Students' Union Target Campaign aims to increase the number of state school applicants as well. The scheme contacts every state sector sixth form in the country, informing them about Target Visits and giving the school the opportunity of receiving a talk from a Cambridge undergraduate about life at Cambridge.

It is very much hoped that all of these schemes will help to dispel some of the myths which surround these two universities.

ETHNIC MINORITY STUDENTS
Cambridge has a group called GEEMA (Group to Encourage Ethnic Minority Applicants) which was formed

to break the image mentioned above and to encourage students from ethnic minorities to apply. The GEEMA coordinator visits schools and colleges and organises open days to help students find out what it is really like at Cambridge from the perspective of an ethnic minority student.

Oxford's Access Scheme exists for a similar purpose and also has a coordinator who works with teachers in schools as well as organising open days and summer schools.

STUDENT PARENTS

The universities welcome applications from students with children and some can offer suitable family accommodation. It is best to ask in advance of your application what they can offer you. Some colleges even have nurseries and there is a Family Society which provides information for student parents. All Cambridge colleges contribute to a bursary scheme which provides funds to parents in financial need.

Cambridge has one university nursery and the following colleges have nursey spaces for the children of their students: Churchill, Girton, Gonville and Caius, Queens', St John's and Trinity.

Oxford has three university nurseries and there are also nurseries at the following colleges: Balliol, Somerville, St Anne's and Wolfson. As at Cambridge, there is a university fund to which applications may be made by those having financial problems in paying for childcare. There are some colleges which offer family accommodation and where this is not possible, the University Accommodation Officer can help in finding private accommodation.

If you have doubts or preconceptions, it is a good idea to attend one of the open days held at the Oxford and Cambridge colleges during the spring and summer terms. Many sixth formers who attend come away with changed minds.

Some teachers too are prejudiced... they have the same illusions of elitism. Many have outdated ideas of what

Oxford and Cambridge are like and others feel that their students would be inadequately prepared to attempt entrance and therefore would be discriminated against.

Oxford and Cambridge are different from other universities. They operate on a different system. They may not appeal to everyone, but they are actively trying to shed their elitist images and they are open to anyone who can meet the entry requirements.

THE COST

The numerous bursaries available at Oxford and Cambridge make them affordable for students from all backgrounds. As for most universities, the annual tuition fee at both Oxford and Cambridge in 2007 will be £3,070. It is no longer necessary for you to pay your tuition fee up front unless you wish to do so. You can choose to defer payment until after you graduate by taking out a loan with the Student Loans Company, who will pay the tuition fee direct to the University on your behalf. You do not start repaying the loan until after you graduate and only then when you are earning more than £15,000 per year.

If you are a UK student, you must apply through your local authority or similar body. Listed below are the places to apply to (or to contact for more information) for students from different regions of the UK and from EU member states.

ENGLAND AND WALES
The appropriate local authority
www.dfes.gov.uk/studentsupport

SCOTLAND
Student Awards Agency for Scotland
Tel: 0131 476 8227
www.student-support-saas.gov.uk

NORTHERN IRELAND
Student Finance NI
Tel: 0845 600 0662
www.studentfinanceni.co.uk

OTHER EU STATE

EU Customer Services Team, Mowden Hall, Staindrop Road, Darlington, United Kingdom DL3 9BG
Tel: +44 141 243 3570

Further information for prospective undergraduates is available in the Department for Education and Skills booklet *Financial Help for Higher Education Students*. You can get this by phoning free on 0800 731 9133.

BURSARIES

It is important to note that both universities run a bursary scheme for those needing financial support. There is also an enormous selection of college and departmental bursaries and/or grants available to help with, for example, travel and book costs as well as general hardship. You should always discuss financial difficulties as soon as possible with your tutor or with the bursar at your college.

2

WHICH SUBJECT?

Your choice of subject is more important than your choice of university and college. Once you have chosen your subject, you should choose your university and then your college. Choice of university and college is dealt with in the next two chapters.

WHY SUBJECT CHOICE IS KEY

First, the emphasis at Oxford and Cambridge is on scholarship. You may be attracted by a subject because of the career prospects that it affords. That's fine. But deep interest in your subject for its own sake, and not merely as a means to an end, is vital if you are going to keep up with the workload and sustain your motivation when the intellectual demands get tough – as they should do and will.

Second, many of the pleasures to be had from your course result from making conceptual breakthroughs and seeing more in the subject than appeared at first sight. You need to be excited when you make these breakthroughs. Otherwise, you'll be missing out on one of the main benefits Oxbridge has to offer.

Third, the entire selection process at Oxford and Cambridge is much more focused on your acumen for a particular subject (as opposed to your general personality) than it is at other universities. Your aptitude is therefore crucial, but the intellectual curiosity that you display for a particular subject can help you through awkward moments in a technical interview. Admissions tutors are people too, and they can't help being positively influenced by candidates who share their passion. Such candidates tend to be nicer to teach. (More on dealing with technical interviews in Chapter 6.)

GETTING STARTED

In short, you're looking for a subject that combines your aptitude and interest. If you already know what the answer is, move on to the next chapter. If not, try the following exercise. It will also help you prepare for your interview.

Start by dividing the courses into lists A, B and C:

A | Courses which appear to be quite different from those commonly offered at A level
B | Courses which appear to build in a slightly more obvious way on some of those studied at A level
C | Courses which appear at first sight to be simple extensions of subjects available at A level.

Note that many of these appearances may be deceptive. Here's one way of carving up the list but it depends, of course, on what subjects are on offer to you at school. (You might, for example, wish to move Psychology, Computing or Law from list A to list C.) Included here are subjects which may be offered singly or in combination.

OXFORD

A | Archaeology and Anthropology; Classical Archaeology and Ancient History; Computer Science; Economics and Management; Experimental Psychology; History of Art; Human Sciences; Law; Oriental Studies; Philosophy; PPE; PPP; Theology
B | Biological Sciences; Earth Sciences; Engineering Science; Materials; Molecular and Cellular Biochemistry; Physiological Sciences and Medicine

C| Chemistry; English; Fine Art; Geography; History;
Literae Humaniores; Mathematics; Modern
Languages; Music; Physics.

CAMBRIDGE

A| Anglo-Saxon, Norse and Celtic Studies; Archaeology
and Anthropology; Architecture; History of Art; Land
Economy; Law; Oriental Studies; Philosophy; Social
and Political Sciences; Theology and Religious Studies

B| Computer Science; Engineering; Medicine; Natural
Sciences; Veterinary Medicine

C| Classics; Economics; English; Geography; History;
Mathematics; Modern and Medieval Languages;
Music.

Now have a look at the course guides in the prospectuses,
paying particular attention to content and A level subject
requirements. The course outlines in the prospectuses
are much more thorough than they used to be and,
whether you are familiar or unfamiliar with Oxford and
Cambridge, they're your best starting point. It's remarkable how many students fall down at interview because
they have not taken the trouble to find out even the most
basic information about their courses from the prospectuses.

To check that you're up to speed on these basics, criticise
the breakdown into Lists A, B and C given above. How
else could it have been carved up? What are the A level
subjects that are apparently being built upon in relevant
list B courses? Why have Chemical Engineering and
Linguistics been omitted from the Cambridge list?
Compare and contrast Oxford and Cambridge for those
interested in the following: Biological Sciences,
Economics, English, Law, Management, Philosophy,
Physics, Politics (see also Chapter 3). Taking seriously
what the prospectuses list as 'advantageous' (as well as
'essential') subjects at A level, start with your A level
combination and list the courses at either university that
appear to have an 'ideal' fit.

GETTING HOLD OF FURTHER INFORMATION

The next step, if you want to be more thorough, is to contact the individual faculties/departments in each university. Remember that, while the college administers the teaching, it is the faculty (ie the subject department within the university) that administers the syllabus. The faculty will have much more detail on course content than is available in the prospectuses and may also have thumbnail sketches of the research interests of the various college fellows. Information about faculty addresses, including website addresses, is available in the prospectuses. Cambridge applicants may also refer to *The Cambridge University Guide to Courses* (Cambridge University Press) or on the website.

If you're wondering whether you're going to be interested in a new subject like Psychology or Computing, or wondering just how much Chemistry there's going to be in Biological Sciences or how much Mathematics in Chemistry, there's no substitute for putting yourself in a first-year undergraduate's shoes. Talk to any undergraduates you know. Look at their lecture notes and essays. Alternatively, get hold of reading lists from the Admissions Tutor's office at your chosen college and take the trouble to do some reading. Don't be afraid to ask. Even if they appear to find your request a bit odd, there are plenty of other people making it. Why not you? For all they know, you're a really strong candidate, with a thirst for extra work, who's choosing between two faculties. The worst they're going to think is that you're being incredibly thorough, and they're very unlikely to make a note of it!

You might be sent the same reading list that successful candidates are asked to work through during the summer holidays before going up to Oxford or Cambridge. That might contain some very general texts which don't relate directly to your future course work. For the first-year undergraduate texts, you might be better off contacting the faculty again. Still no luck? Take the trouble to visit the university again one Saturday and spend the afternoon in the university bookshop (Blackwell's in Oxford or Heffers in Cambridge). The staff are very familiar with the books that are used by undergraduates.

CHECKLIST

- ☐ Research course content in prospectuses
- ☐ Analyse fit with A levels
- ☐ Contact faculties departments for fellows' research interests
- ☐ Talk to current undergraduates
- ☐ Get hold of the reading lists
- ☐ Visit the bookshops.

3

WHICH UNIVERSITY?

You've found an optimum combination of aptitude
and interest and you've chosen your subject. But
it's one of those subjects that you could read at
either university. You're aware of many of the vari-
ations of approach from the research that you did
when choosing your subject, but you'd be pretty
happy with either university, and you need to
have something up your sleeve if you're asked
'Why Oxford?' or 'Why Cambridge?'

**GENERAL
CONSIDERA-
TIONS**

You need to draw a distinction between perfectly reasonable bases for choosing a particular university, and what
you can get away with saying at interview.

Geographical considerations, recommendations by family,
friends or school, the presence or absence of friends and
relatives already studying there, or a special predilection
for a particular college are all reasonable bases (after all
it's a personal choice) and could be cited briefly and with
relative impunity at interview.

Subtleties of course content, flexibility v specialisation,
and subject combination options can be key criteria and
may certainly be brought up. So sometimes can extracur-

ricular considerations if you're sure of your ground. It's probably not a very good idea to say that you prefer Cambridge because it's close to the racing mecca of Newmarket, but perhaps more legitimate to say that you think that you have a greater chance of getting a rowing blue at Oxford (a *blue* means representing the university in a particular sport).

The desire to work under a particular college fellow or to witness the lectures of a particular university professor might be admirable criteria if you know what you're talking about. Some of the intellectual luminaries of yesteryear chose their university on that basis. Beware, though. There could be real problems if you don't know enough about their fields and you could become deflated at interview if told that your guru has left the university now, no longer teaches undergraduates or is on sabbatical for a year.

'Reputation' is strongly advised against as either a disclosed or undisclosed criterion. In the first place, academic research strengths in particular departments are much more important in postgraduate than in undergraduate work. Second, it would be naive to think that either university is 'better' (though it's amazing how many — usually unsuccessful — applicants mention it at interview). This often betrays an insufficiently critical analysis of newspaper league tables. Third, your interviewers may have connections at both Oxford and Cambridge and have as much fondness for their old undergraduate university as the one in which they now work, if not more. Value judgements about the tutorial v supervision systems can be equally risky. The similarities between the two systems far outweigh the differences, and neither university wants to hear a school leaver pontificating about which system delivers the 'better' education.

You're likely to be on strongest ground when talking about course content and course flexibility (or, conversely, specialisation). It shows that you've researched your subject and that, as we've said before, is more important than anything bar your academic acumen. Let's look at the similarities and differences of general approach.

CAMBRIDGE

It is often said that one of the great attractions of Cambridge is the flexibility of its Tripos system. The name Tripos is said to be derived from the three-legged stool that undergraduates in medieval times would sit on for their oral examinations.

Each course, or Tripos, is usually divided into two parts, Parts I and II. It's quite easy to understand how Part I works. It's taken after either one year (eg Economics) or two years (eg English). Often, a two-year Part I is divided into IA and IB with examinations at the end of each of the first two years (eg Geography). The real flexibility kicks in following the successful completion of Part I. One obvious option is to specialise further by completing Part II in the same Tripos. For three-year courses, if Part I takes two years, Part II takes one year and vice versa. However, many students switch Tripos after Part I, sometimes involving a one-year Part II, sometimes a two-year Part II.

Switching of Tripos is one way of ending up with a four-year undergraduate course. In addition, Natural Science and Mathematics students have the option of adding a Part III, while Engineering students take Parts IA, IB, IIA and IIB over four years, leading ultimately to the award of MEng.

OXFORD

Arts students normally take an examination during their first year which they must pass in order to continue the degree. These examinations are known as Prelims (pre-liminary examinations) but they do not count towards the final degree mark. At the end of the final year, arts students will take exams known as Finals (Final Honour School). These take place over a period of two weeks but some may be replaced by a thesis and/or extended written work.

Science students also take Prelims at the end of the first year and, as with the Arts examinations, these must be passed in order to progress on the course. Finals are taken at the end of the third year but some will sit them at the end of the second year. Some of these examinations may be replaced by a project or a dissertation. The fourth year of science degrees (most science degrees last for four years) may be entirely research based but some courses will also have examinations.

In general there are rather more courses at Oxford that are designed to take (rather than having the option of taking) four years. The joint honours courses of Mathematics and Philosophy and Physics and Philosophy, as well as Classics, take four years. Mathematics itself, Physics and Earth Sciences can take either three or four years (your choice) but, in the case of Molecular and Cellular Biochemistry, Chemistry, Engineering and Metallurgy, students would normally be expected to progress to the fourth, research-based year leading to the award of the Masters degree.

SIMILARITIES AND DIFFERENCES

On balance, the two universities have converged rather than diverged in recent years and you should not over-state the differences at interview.

Where Cambridge has the flexibility of its Tripos system, Oxford has more in the way of joint honours courses. For years, Archaeology and Anthropology was offered only at Cambridge. Now it is offered at Oxford too. Keep the differences that remain clearly in focus – lots of courses in Cambridge with exams each year; individual differences between three- and four-year options at the two universities; no real equivalent to SPS available at Oxford; no real equivalent to PPE available at Cambridge; less ability to specialise in a single Science subject at Cambridge; no facility for studying Economics or Philosophy as a single subject at Oxford; no facility for studying Psychology as a single subject at Cambridge. Research the similarities and differences as they apply to your particular subject choice and don't forget what you have discovered when it comes to interview.

CHECKLIST

- [ ] Remember that course comes first
- [ ] Research subtleties of course content
- [ ] Weigh up any personal, geographical or extracurricular considerations
- [ ] Weigh up differences in academic approach.

4

WHICH COLLEGE?

HOW TO CHOOSE A COLLEGE

The best advice to help you choose a college is to go to the universities and visit as many of the colleges as you can. Use the open days and if you are unable to make those dates, call the college admissions tutor and ask if you can have a look around. When you are there, try to talk to as many people as possible; the students and the porters are a great source of information on what will become important topics to you such as: What are the rooms like? What is the food in Halls like? Is the library open 24 hours? Ask the undergraduates why they applied there and if they are enjoying it. Remember too that if you have visited the college which you eventually apply for, you can discuss this at interview if you are asked why you applied. That is one less question to worry about when it comes to the big day!

When you do make your application you can specify a college of your choice, but if you really cannot decide you may make an open application which means that you have no preference. Each university has slightly different processes with regard to the application.

CAMBRIDGE

You may apply to one specific college to which you send your application form. If you are unsuccessful in your application and subsequent interview you may be placed in the Winter Pool, which is designed to ensure that the best applicants are offered places. Where the college you have applied to was oversubscribed they may, if they feel your application was strong, 'pool' your application for other colleges to consider. You may then find that you are called for interview by a college you did not apply for. If they require an interview with you it will take place in mid-January and you will hear the result soon afterwards. There is also a small Summer Pool which takes place after the A level results have been published.

You may also make an open application to Cambridge – in this case the admissions computer will allocate your application to a college and your application will be treated in exactly the same way as if you had specifically applied to that college. The university states that open applications do as well as applications to a specific college so you should not worry that you will be disadvantaged.

Oxford
Like Cambridge you may apply to one specific college of your choice. The main difference is that you are also automatically allocated second and third preference colleges and it is not possible to change these. Again you may also make an open application where you will be allocated a college of first preference.

Why choose a specific college?
If you do not choose a college you may find yourself allocated to one you do not like. You may wish to consider the following when choosing your college:

- Whether mixed or single sex
- Religious character (where applicable)
- Architecture
- Financial assistance available
- Facilities (eg for socialising or sport)
- Quality and quantity of accommodation
- Societies and sports clubs
- Proximity to city centre
- Proximity to faculty

- Number of other students in your subject
- Academic results and reputation of research fellows
- First impressions.

You may decide that you would prefer to be in a college where there will be plenty of other students to talk to who are doing your subject. This is a perfectly acceptable reason for choosing a college. Students learn from and can be motivated by each other. Likewise, if you're a mature student, you may prefer one of the colleges that admits a good number of mature students or exclusively admits mature students.

If you've done your homework, not only will you have chosen a college that's right for you but you will also have an informed, interesting, articulate and acceptable answer to the 'why?' question if you're asked it at interview.

IS IT EASIER TO GET INTO CERTAIN COLLEGES?

Students often spend hours poring over the prospectuses and statistics trying to work out which college is the easiest to get an offer from for each subject. There are even companies which will charge you a fee for suggesting a number of colleges for you to target by looking at the history of competition for places. If you are tempted to pay for such a service, have a look in the prospectus before you part with your cash as you will find the answers you need there. You can also get your answers on the websites and even by contacting the college admissions offices. Note also that although a certain college may have had only 15 applications for Theology last year, how on earth do you know that the statistics will remain the same this year when you apply? Add to that the fact that if lots of other people are paying for someone to select their college on this basis, surely the number of applications will rise thereby making the whole process void. Do not pay too much attention to the history of entry statistics (although some statistics have been included here for fullness of information) but do have a look at some of the following.

STRATEGIC CONSIDERATIONS

You may also be influenced in your choice by strategic considerations. In other words, you may wish to pick a college not because you like its special features, but because you feel that you have a better chance of being admitted there.

ADMISSIONS CRITERIA

One strategy in choosing a college is to consider the method the colleges use to assess you.

See Chapter 5 for further advice on the submission of written work before interview and more detail on the written tests. The colleges in both universities have similar admissions criteria. There may, however, be slight differences in terms of written tests and work submitted.

APPLICANTS FROM YOUR OWN SCHOOL

Another consideration can come into the equation if you have lots of competitors from your own school all converging on the same college. (Typically, this will apply only to a small number of the largest independent schools) In theory, this should be irrelevant – colleges would argue that admission is entirely meritocratic after the point of application. However, if you feel that you are worthy of a place but that you are definitely not among the strongest of a very strong entry from your school, you may decide that it would be wiser to play the strategic card and apply elsewhere – but only if you are happy to do so.

INTEREST IN COLLEGE FELLOW'S SPECIALISATION

Strategy can come into play if you happen to have done a lot of reading on an area that is of special interest to your subject interviewer. This is another reason why it's a good idea to get hold of that faculty list. Suppose, for example, that you can't decide on your college, but you're applying to read Experimental Psychology at Oxford and know a lot about Social Psychology. You might be drawn to a college where the Psychology fellow specialises in that field for the simple reason that you are going to come across better at interview if you can turn the conversation in that direction. Similar considerations might come into play in English, History, History of Art or Geography. A word of caution, though: you're not always interviewed by the person you're expecting.

HOW TO GO ABOUT IT

■ Visit the university at least once and preferably twice. Colleges hold open days between April and July and also in September (details in prospectuses).

■ Visit any friends who are studying at the university, visit the bookshops, cafes etc. Get a feel for the place.

■ Apply the considerations listed under 'Why choose a specific college?'

■ Apply any strategic consideration as detailed above.

■ Check the thumbnail sketches in this book and university prospectuses.

■ Draw up a shortlist and obtain the college prospectuses. Read faculty literature and look at the research interests of the fellows. Be sure to filter out fields of research that have nothing to do with the undergraduate curriculum.

■ Investigate the research interests of the fellows.

■ Make your final decision or, if you cannot, make an open application.

The next part of this chapter is devoted to thumbnail sketches of the Oxford and Cambridge colleges admitting undergraduates. Use this only as your starting point. The tables on pages 63–84 give you some idea of the number of students reading each subject at each college.

OXFORD UNDER-GRADUATE COLLEGES

For English and PPE, the Oxford colleges operate in groups for admissions purposes. Your second and third preference colleges will always come from the same group as your first preference college if you are applying for one of the subjects to which the group system applies.

The groups are:

GROUP 1
Brasenose, Christ Church, Jesus, Lincoln, Magdalen, Mansfield, Merton, Oriel, St Hilda's, Somerville

GROUP 2
Balliol, Exeter, Keble, Pembroke, St Anne's, St Edmund Hall, St John's, St Peter's, Wadham

GROUP 3
Corpus Christi, Harris Manchester, Hertford, Lady
Margaret Hall, New College, Queen's, St Catherine's, St
Hugh's, Trinity, University, Worcester

PERMANENT PRIVATE HALLS
Blackfriars, Campion Hall, Greyfriars, Regent's Park
College, St Benet's Hall, St Stephen's House, Wycliffe Hall

Although PPHs do not have the status of full colleges of
the university, students admitted by them are members of
the university. Some have restrictions on entry. For admissions procedures, see individual descriptions.

Please note that the figure given for the number of students at each college may vary slightly from year to year.

BALLIOL COLLEGE
Founded: 1263.
Students: 422 undergraduates; undergraduate
male–female ratio: 3–2.
Position: Central, just off Broad Street.
Buildings: An interesting mix of styles – 15th to 20th
centuries, including a famous Victorian chapel.
Library: Large library, open 24 hours.
Accommodation: Guaranteed in college for two years.
Facilities include: Tennis and squash courts; multigym;
boathouse; sports ground centrally placed close to college.
Other features include: Known for welcoming under-
graduates from overseas.

BLACKFRIARS
Founded: A theological college since 1922; a permanent
private hall since 1 January 1994.
Students: 16 undergraduates; undergraduate
male–female ratio: 3–1.
Position: St Giles.
Buildings: 18th-century exterior; main buildings 1920s.
Quad and gardens.
Library: Large library of theology books, open
8.30am–10pm.

Accommodation: Only available to members of the Dominican order.

Other features include: Strong preference for mature students.

BRASENOSE COLLEGE
Founded: 1509.

Students: 362 undergraduates; undergraduate male–female ratio: 4–3.

Position: Very central position, with detached Frewin Quad some three minutes' walk away.

Buildings: Attractive, homogenous mix of Tudor, Jacobean and late Victorian Gothic.

Library: Three libraries with a key system for night opening.

Accommodation: Available for all 1st and 2nd years and for most 3rd year undergraduates.

Facilities include: Sports ground with squash and tennis courts, half a mile away; boathouse.

Other features include: The college has the reputation of being friendly and close-knit.

Known as: BNC.

CAMPION HALL
Founded: 1896.

Students: 1 undergraduate; all male. This is the Jesuits' academic hall in Oxford, but not all students are Jesuits. Priests and members of other religious orders are admitted as well as a very small number of laymen.

Position: In central Oxford, opposite Pembroke College.

Buildings: A fine Lutyens building, recently extended.

Library: Open 24 hours.

Accommodation: Available to all undergraduates.

Other features include: Relaxed and friendly atmosphere.

CHRIST CHURCH
Founded: 1546.

Students: 426 undergraduates; undergraduate male–female ratio: 4–3.

Position: Just south of centre, easy access to the Meadows and river.

Buildings: Grand and majestic, architecturally Christ Church is one of the most impressive in Oxford. The Great Quadrangle is dominated by Wren's 'Tom Tower', an Oxford landmark, over the gatehouse. The magnificent chapel is the city's cathedral.

Library: Very large library in superb 18th-century building; modern Law library.

Accommodation: College accommodation for all years.

Facilities include: Fine music room; cathedral has one of Britain's finest organs; squash and tennis courts; boathouse; sports ground a few minutes away and reached by ferry; picture gallery.

Other features include: Flourishing music life.

Known as: The House.

CORPUS CHRISTI COLLEGE

Founded: 1517.

Students: 246 undergraduates; undergraduate male–female ratio: 4–3.

Position: Just off High Street, but with direct access to the river.

Buildings: Fine panelled Hall with original hammer-beam roof and the magnificent 17th-century Old Library.

Library: Large library, open 24 hours.

Accommodation: College accommodation for all years.

Facilities include: Squash court; modern boathouse; sports ground some 15 minutes' walk away; music room.

Other features include: Small size of college, giving an intimate and warm atmosphere.

EXETER COLLEGE

Founded: 1314.

Students: 328 undergraduates; undergraduate male–female ratio: 6–5.

Position: In the centre, next to the Bodleian Library and near University Science Area.

Buildings: Compact quads with most buildings dating from 17th to 20th centuries – of particular note are the Victorian chapel and fine 17th-century dining hall.

Library: Large library, open 24 hours.

Accommodation: Most undergraduates can be offered a full three years' accommodation in college and college houses, flats or hostels.

Facilities include: Sports ground some 20 minutes away; multigym in college; boathouse.

Other features include: Small compact site which encourages friendly and lively college activities.

GREYFRIARS

Founded: 1224. Refounded 1910.

Students: 31 undergraduates; undergraduate male–female ratio: 3–2. This is the Franciscans' academic hall in Oxford, but not all students are Franciscans. Priests and members of other religious orders are admitted as well as a very small number of laymen.

Position: Down the Iffley Road in the east of Oxford.

Buildings: Attractive 1930s Friary building.

Library: Open 24 hours.

Accommodation: Available to all undergraduates.

Facilities include: Computer room.

Other features include: Strong sports links with the university.

HARRIS MANCHESTER COLLEGE

Founded: 1786.

Students: 108 undergraduates; undergraduate male–female ratio: 5–6. Admits only mature students, from the age of 21.

Position: Central, close to Bodleian Library and Science Departments.

Buildings: Handsome Victorian Gothic revival buildings. Chapel with fine Burne-Jones stained glass windows. New classical quad.

Library: Open 8am–11pm.

Accommodation: Available for three years for all those wishing to live in. Guaranteed for at least the first and final years.

Facilities include: Sports facilities shared with other colleges.

Other features include: College situated centrally, close to all university facilities. Informal atmosphere congenial both for study and social activities. Candidates may name Harris Manchester as first or second choice on Oxford application form.

HERTFORD COLLEGE
Founded: 1282.
Students: 370 undergraduates; undergraduate male–female ratio: 1–1.
Position: Central position, facing the Bodleian Library.
Buildings: Three quads, mainly 19th century, but some buildings date back to 16th century. The best-known feature is the bridge over the lane which divides the college.
Library: Open 24 hours.
Accommodation: Available for all undergraduates in college or college houses.
Facilities include: Sports ground; boathouse; multigym.
Other features include: Compact site; very high intake from state sector; over 20 years' experience of offering places without examination.

JESUS COLLEGE
Founded: 1571.
Students: 330 undergraduates; undergraduate male–female ratio: 6–5.
Position: Right in the heart of the city and university.
Buildings: Compact quads, some buildings date from 16th century, and inner quad is notable for its fine proportions. Substantial 20th-century additions.
Library: Open long hours.
Accommodation: College accommodation for all years.
Facilities include: Large music room; squash courts; sports field; modern boathouse; multigym; darkroom.
Other features include: Close-knit site; historic link with Wales.

KEBLE COLLEGE
Founded: 1870.
Students: 422 undergraduates; undergraduate male–female ratio: 5–4.

Position: Opposite University Parks and near science departments.

Buildings: Famous and distinctive Victorian structure in coloured bricks – the massive chapel is a masterpiece. Large modern extension.

Library: Large library, open 24 hours.

Accommodation: All 1st and 2nd years accommodated plus many 3rd years, in modern or modernised rooms.

Facilities include: Squash courts; boathouse; sports ground; modern computer room.

Other features include: High Anglican tradition. Flourishing sporting and musical life.

LADY MARGARET HALL

Founded: 1878.

Students: 400 undergraduates; undergraduate male–female ratio: 1–1.

Position: In 11 beautiful acres of gardens beside the River Cherwell to north of the city centre.

Buildings: Substantial 19th- and 20th-century buildings, quietly set.

Library: Large library, open 24 hours; separate Law library.

Accommodation: Available for all 1st and 2nd years, and for most 3rd years.

Facilities include: Boathouse shared with Trinity; squash court; music facilities.

Other features include: Now co-residential, was the first academic hall founded for women at Oxford.

Known as: LMH.

LINCOLN COLLEGE

Founded: 1427.

Students: 303 undergraduates; undergraduate male–female ratio: 5–4.

Position: In the heart of the city, just north of High Street.

Buildings: Unspoilt medieval buildings sit cheek by jowl with a fine Queen Anne church, now the elegant library. Famous medieval Mitre Inn across road, now taken over and extended and incorporated into college.

Library: Open until late.

Accommodation: The college offers accommodation to all undergraduates.

Facilities include: Boathouse, multigym, squash court, sports ground.

Other features include: Strong sense of community in a small college noted for friendliness.

MAGDALEN COLLEGE

Founded: 1458.

Students: 389 undergraduates; undergraduate male–female ratio: 6–5.

Position: In extensive grounds beside the river at east end of the High Street.

Buildings: Romantic late medieval buildings including fine 15th-century cloisters and the famous Great Tower, a notable Oxford landmark (choir sings from top of tower on May Day morning).

Library: Large library (in three buildings), open 24 hours.

Accommodation: Available on site or nearby for all undergraduates who want rooms.

Facilities include: Tennis and squash courts; boathouse and punts; riverside sports ground; new auditorium; dark room.

Other features include: Particularly spacious grounds including lovely gardens, deer park, etc. One of largest colleges, Magdalen (pronounced *maudlin*) has a fine musical tradition.

MANSFIELD COLLEGE

Founded: 1886.

Students: 191 undergraduates; undergraduate male–female ratio: 3–2.

Position: Quietly set in north-west corner of city centre, close to Bodleian Library and Science Departments.

Buildings: Fine Victorian and later buildings.

Library: Open 24 hours.

Accommodation: Available to all 1st years and 3rd years.

Facilities include: Sports facilities shared with Merton nearby.

Other features include: Mansfield, originally a Free Church foundation, is now a full college; it received its Royal Charter in 1995. It has a spacious site close to all the libraries and shops. A small college with a friendly environment.

MERTON COLLEGE
Founded: 1264.
Students: 309 undergraduates; undergraduate male–female ratio: 3–2.
Position: Overlooks Christ Church Meadow in central but quiet site.
Buildings: Contains, in Mob quad, the oldest surviving quadrangle in Oxford – 14th century. A beautiful group of medieval and later buildings.
Library: Large historic library open until late. Separate Science and Law libraries.
Accommodation: Available for all undergraduates.
Facilities include: Sports ground close to college; tennis and squash courts; boathouse.
Other features include: Particularly beautiful garden bordered by the City Wall; drama and music traditions.

NEW COLLEGE
Founded: 1379.
Students: 420 undergraduates; undergraduate male–female ratio: 6–5.
Position: Centrally placed beside City Wall.
Buildings: Despite its name, New College boasts some fine medieval buildings including cloisters, chapel, hall and front quadrangle. Also fine 17th-century buildings and recent additions.
Library: Large library; open until midnight.
Accommodation: All students may be accommodated for their first two years in college; many accommodated for 3rd year.
Facilities include: Riverside sports ground close to college; boathouse; tennis and squash courts.
Other features include: Music tradition (famous chapel choir, undergraduate orchestra, choir, etc); one of the largest colleges in Oxford.

ORIEL COLLEGE

Founded: 1326.

Students: 304 undergraduates; undergraduate male–female ratio: 3–2.

Position: Near Carfax right in the middle of Oxford.

Buildings: Compact group of fine medieval and later buildings. One of few colleges with no post-war buildings on its main site.

Library: Large and beautiful Senior Library; charming Junior Library, open 24 hours; almost all book requests are purchased.

Accommodation: Consists of a variety of styles (single rooms, sets, flats and cottages) on the main site, the adjacent Island site (linked by under-road tunnel) and the Rectory Road annexe. All undergraduates are accommodated throughout their courses, including any retake years.

Facilities include: Squash court; two multigyms; sports ground; boathouse.

Other features include: Small size; Formal Hall six nights a week; domination of the river for most of the last few decades; first college of royal foundation in Oxford or Cambridge; full name is 'The House of Blessed Mary the Virgin in Oxford, commonly called Oriel College'.

PEMBROKE COLLEGE

Founded: 1624.

Students: 416 undergraduates; undergraduate male–female ratio: 3–2.

Position: Just south of the city centre.

Buildings: Mixture of attractive ancient and modern buildings on a relatively small site plus a major new (1988) residential building a few minutes' walk away beside the Isis.

Library: Open until late.

Accommodation: Available for most undergraduates.

Facilities include: Squash and tennis courts; sports ground; boathouse.

Other features include: Compact site of college; first college to begin a JCR art collection to support emerging artists.

THE QUEEN'S COLLEGE
Founded: 1341.
Students: 304 undergraduates; undergraduate male–female ratio: 1–1.
Position: Right on the High Street.
Buildings: Based on two imposing 17th- to 18th-century quadrangles designed by Wren and Hawksmoor. Particularly fine Upper Library. Modern additions include dramatic Florey Building across Magdalen Bridge.
Library: Very large library.
Accommodation: College accommodation for all years.
Facilities include: Tennis and squash courts; shared boathouse; large sports ground; concert piano.
Other features include: Music tradition; Frobenius organ.

REGENT'S PARK COLLEGE
Founded: 1810.
Students: 84 undergraduates; undergraduate male–female ratio: 1–1. Founded as a Baptist college, priority is given to applicants wishing to become Baptist Ministers, but a small number of other students are admitted annually in subjects other than Theology.
Position: Central site, just off St Giles'.
Buildings: Compact clean-lined buildings, 1920s and later.
Library: Open 24 hours.
Accommodation: Most students accommodated.
Other features include: Several sports teams.

ST ANNE'S COLLEGE
Founded: 1879.
Students: 437 undergraduates; undergraduate male–female ratio: 1–1.
Position: Close to the Parks, three-quarters of a mile north of city centre.
Buildings: A pleasing mix of Victorian houses, 1930s and 1960s buildings and the attractive main structure by Giles Gilbert Scott.
Library: Open long hours.
Accommodation: Available for all 1st and 3rd years and most 2nd years.

Facilities include: Sports ground shared with St John's; boathouse.

Other features include: Originated as college for home study for women students; now a mixed college enjoying considerable sporting success.

ST BENET'S HALL

Founded: 1897.

Students: 45 undergraduates; all male. Welcomes monks from all over the world, although majority of undergraduates are laymen.

Position: Central, on St Giles'.

Buildings: A fine extended Georgian town house.

Library: Open 24 hours.

Accommodation: Most students housed.

Facilities include: Croquet lawn.

Other features include: Majority are Catholic but other traditions are welcome.

ST CATHERINE'S COLLEGE

Founded: 1963.

Students: 447 undergraduates; undergraduate male–female ratio: 3–2.

Position: Quietly set beside Cherwell in east of centre, but within easy reach of all university facilities.

Buildings: Dramatic moated 1960s structure – light, airy and spacious.

Library: Large library open until late.

Accommodation: All undergraduates guaranteed two years in college, possibly three.

Facilities include: Squash and tennis courts; sports ground nearby; lecture and film theatre; Music House (for concerts etc) in grounds.

Other features include: One of the largest colleges – and is the only completely modern undergraduate college in Oxford.

Known as: St Catz.

ST EDMUND HALL

Founded: c 1278.

Students: 400 undergraduates; undergraduate male–female ratio: 3–2.

Position: Centrally placed off eastern end of High Street.
Buildings: College has grown from a small, intimate medieval quad and now includes a large beautiful Norman church (converted to the library) and substantial additions including a modern block by the Parks.
Library: Open 16 hours a day.
Accommodation: Almost all undergraduates accommodated for three years.
Facilities include: Multigym; tennis courts; boathouse.
Other features include: JCR has an introductory programme for newly arrived undergraduates; known for sport.
Known as: Teddy Hall

St Hilda's College
Founded: 1893.
Students: 419 undergraduates; currently all female, but this is due to change in the next few years.
Position: In fine large gardens beside the Cherwell just east of Magdalen Bridge.
Buildings: Range of 18th- to 20th-century buildings.
Library: 24-hour access.
Accommodation: Undergraduates guaranteed accommodation for at least two years.
Facilities include: Punts; tennis court; musical facilities.
Other features include: Remarkably open and quiet situation despite central position; the famous gardens have many rare plants. College has strong international links, encouraging travel overseas and welcoming visiting foreign students.

St Hugh's College
Founded: 1886.
Students: 419 undergraduates; undergraduate male–female ratio: 4–3.
Position: In North Oxford but in easy reach of university facilities.
Buildings: A mix of neo-Georgian and modern buildings, with some fine Victorian houses, spaciously set in 14 acres of grounds.

Library: Open 24 hours.
Accommodation: Available on site for three years.
Facilities include: Tennis courts; very large and attractive gardens.
Other features include: Strong musical tradition.

ST JOHN'S COLLEGE
Founded: 1555.
Students: 397 undergraduates; undergraduate male–female ratio: 6–5.
Position: Right in the centre of the city.
Buildings: A lovely mixture of buildings – its 17th-century quadrangle is considered an architectural *tour de force* and the garden, containing England's oldest rock garden, is justly famous.
Library: Large library; open late.
Accommodation: Available for all undergraduates.
Facilities include: Squash and all-weather tennis courts; weights room; boathouse; sports ground about a mile away; art gallery; auditorium.
Other features include: This is Oxford's most richly endowed college. Fine musical tradition.

ST PETER'S COLLEGE
Founded: 1929.
Students: 390 undergraduates; undergraduate male–female ratio: 3–2.
Position: In west of city centre.
Buildings: An interesting mixture including a former Georgian rectory, a former medieval hall and church and several 19th- to 20th-century buildings including a 1980s quadrangle.
Library: Open all day.
Accommodation: Available for 1st years and 3rd years and some 2nd years.
Facilities include: Squash courts; boathouse; sports ground, some two miles away; law centre.

ST STEPHEN'S HOUSE
Founded: 1876.
Students: 30 undergraduates; undergraduate male–female ratio: 5–1

Position: In the heart of East Oxford, opposite university sports ground.

Buildings: Recently refurbished monastery of the Society of St John the Evangelist.

Library: Major theological library; open all day.

Accommodation: All students and their families are housed.

Facilities include: Secluded gardens; quiet cloisters; bar.

Other features include: Friendly and supportive atmosphere for students and their families; many mature students over 25.

SOMERVILLE COLLEGE

Founded: 1879.

Students: 370 undergraduates; undergraduate male–female ratio: 1–1.

Position: Just north of city centre, off Woodstock Road.

Buildings: Fine 19th-century buildings, and modern additions, set in surprising amount of space for such a central location.

Library: Large library, open 24 hours.

Accommodation: All 1st and 3rd years – and some 2nd years – accommodated.

Facilities include: Tennis courts; punts; music facilities, etc.

Other features include: Known for its relaxed and friendly atmosphere.

TRINITY COLLEGE

Founded: 1554.

Students: 297 undergraduates; undergraduate male–female ratio: 6–5.

Position: In Broad Street, centrally placed.

Buildings: Close-knit college stretching back from road – includes medieval and modern buildings as well as a Wren chapel.

Library: Open 24 hours.

Accommodation: Available for all three years.

Facilities include: Sports ground; boathouse (shared with Magdalen); squash court.

Other features include: Large chamber orchestra; large 'hidden' college garden with wide lawns.

UNIVERSITY COLLEGE
Founded: 1249.
Students: 420 undergraduates; undergraduate male–female undergraduate ratio: 3–2.
Position: Central position on the High Street.
Buildings: Attractive range of buildings dating from 16th century to the present day. Annexe of Victorian and modern buildings in north Oxford.
Library: Two libraries, open 24 hours.
Accommodation: Available to all undergraduates.
Facilities include: Squash court; boathouse; sports ground.
Other features include: Oldest college in the university; strong sporting, music and drama traditions.
Known as: Univ.

WADHAM COLLEGE
Founded: 1610.
Students: 480 undergraduates; undergraduate male–female ratio: 5–6.
Position: Central position opposite the Bodleian Library.
Buildings: Main feature is the fine Jacobean quadrangle, but there are major modern additions from the 1950s–1980s.
Library: Large modern library, open 24 hours.
Accommodation: Available for 1st years and 3rd years plus some 2nd years.
Facilities include: Squash court; sports ground; weight room; boathouse; theatre.
Other features include: Strong musical tradition. Relatively large for an Oxford college.

WORCESTER COLLEGE
Founded: 1714.
Students: 413 undergraduates; undergraduate male–female ratio: 6–5.
Position: On western fringe of city centre – the only college near to the railway station.

Buildings: A fine mixture ranging from picturesque 15th-century former Gloucester College through the 18th-century chapel, hall and library to a 1980s block.
Library: Two libraries, open 24 hours.
Accommodation: Available to all 1st and 2nd years plus most 3rd years.
Facilities include: Tennis and squash courts; boathouse; the only on-site sports ground of any Oxford college.
Other features include: 26 acres of grounds including a very fine garden and beautiful lake; famous dramatic society puts on regular performances in the garden.

WYCLIFFE HALL
Founded: 1877.
Students: 76, male–female undergraduate ratio: 3–1.
Position: North Oxford close to the parks.
Accommodation: Available to all 1st, and most 2nd and 3rd, years.
Facilities include: Theological library; computer room.
Other features include: Family atmosphere with a large proportion of married students with children.

OXFORD GRADUATE COLLEGES

The following colleges do not admit undergraduates:

- All Souls College
- Green College
- Kellogg College
- Linacre College
- Nuffield College
- St Anthony's College
- St Cross College
- Templeton College
- Wolfson College.

CAMBRIDGE UNDER-GRADUATE COLLEGES

CHRIST'S COLLEGE
Founded: 1505.
Students: 395 undergraduates; undergraduate male–female ratio: 3–2.
Position: Perhaps the most centrally placed of Cambridge colleges.

Buildings: Its four courts include a notably picturesque 15th-century First Court and some striking modern buildings.

Library: Modern library open 24 hours; separate Law library.

Accommodation: Available for all undergraduates.

Facilities include: Sports facilities including squash courts; theatre.

Other features include: No shared accommodation; medieval dining hall.

CHURCHILL COLLEGE

Founded: 1960.

Students: 450 undergraduates; undergraduate male–female ratio: 3–2.

Position: The largest college site in Cambridge, Churchill is about a mile out of the city centre.

Buildings: Spacious 1960s buildings arranged around traditional Cambridge courts.

Library: Open 24 hours.

Accommodation: Available to all undergraduates for three years.

Facilities include: Sports ground on site; tennis and squash courts; theatre and exhibition hall.

Other features include: One of the largest colleges in Cambridge; it admits more scientists and engineers than any other. The college has a very high state school intake.

CLARE COLLEGE

Founded: 1326.

Students: 440 undergraduates; undergraduate male–female ratio: 1–1.

Position: Very close to the city centre, with separate Memorial Court across the river.

Buildings: 17th-century Old Court makes an elegant focal point for this group of fine buildings with lovely grounds beside the Cam.

Library: New Library – open from very early morning until midnight.

Accommodation: Available to all undergraduates.

Facilities include: Squash courts; music, photography, studio and pottery rooms, etc; sports ground over a mile away

Other features include: College is on either side of the river, linked by a bridge; outstanding gardens.

CORPUS CHRISTI COLLEGE

Founded: 1352.

Students: 250 undergraduates; undergraduate male–female ratio: 3–2.

Position: Compact college centrally placed off King's Parade.

Buildings: Old Court, built in 14th century, is oldest continuously used court in Cambridge; New Court is a fine group of 1820s buildings.

Library: Key system for 24-hour access.

Accommodation: Available to all undergraduates for three years.

Facilities include: Tennis and squash courts, boathouse; garden with swimming pool by sports ground.

Other features include: One of the smallest colleges in Cambridge; Parker Library of early books.

Known as: Corpus.

DOWNING COLLEGE

Founded: 1800.

Students: 403 undergraduates; undergraduate male–female ratio: 5–4.

Position: Large site at southern edge of city centre.

Buildings: Impressive neo-Classical architecture on a grand scale – chapel and Regency dining hall and new Howard Building, which comprises public rooms, also new library, are particularly notable.

Library: Open until 11.30pm.

Accommodation: All undergraduates are guaranteed at least two years in college.

Facilities include: Tennis and squash courts on site; sports ground a mile away; boathouse.

Other features include: Very substantial grounds (16 acres).

EMMANUEL COLLEGE

Founded: 1584.

Students: 469 undergraduates; undergraduate male–female ratio: 1–1.

Position: In city centre, near to major university departments and laboratories.

Buildings: A dignified group of buildings including a magnificent Wren chapel and new building by Hopkins.

Library: Open late, evenings and weekends.

Accommodation: Available for all three years; hostel or college house accommodation for 2nd years.

Facilities include: Boathouse; squash and tennis courts; swimming pool; sports ground; chapel organ, harpsichord and grand piano; video equipment; computer room; theatre.

Other features include: A large and beautiful garden containing duck ponds and fine trees.

Known as: Emma.

FITZWILLIAM COLLEGE

Founded: 1966.

Students: 474 undergraduates; undergraduate male–female ratio: 3–2.

Position: Off the Huntingdon Road about a mile northwest of city centre.

Buildings: College moved into brand new buildings in the 1960s – largely brick-built on an open site.

Library: Open until 2am; large Law collection.

Accommodation: Undergraduates guaranteed accommodation for two years.

Facilities include: Sports ground nearby; squash courts; boathouse.

Other features include: Particularly high intake from the state sector.

Known as: Fitz.

GIRTON COLLEGE

Founded: 1869.

Students: 503 undergraduates; undergraduate male–female ratio: 1–1.

Position: Very large site, some two miles north-west of city centre.

Buildings: An impressive set of red-brick Victorian buildings set in 50 acres of gardens, woods and meadows; includes modern Wolfson Court near city centre.

Library: Large library open until 11 pm.

Accommodation: Available to all undergraduates.

Facilities include: Sports ground, tennis and squash courts, swimming pool, etc on site; boathouse; bicycle repair shop.

Other features include: Founded as the first women's college in Cambridge; all Girton students may take meals at Wolfson Court in city centre. Over 60% of the students are from state schools.

Gonville and Caius College

Founded: 1348, re-founded 1558.

Students: 475 undergraduates; undergraduate male–female ratio: 5–4.

Position: College in two parts – one right in city centre; the other next to University Library across the river.

Buildings: Attractive Tudor buildings next to University Church – the Gate of Virtue is much photographed; 1960s Harvey Court separate site.

Library: Open 24 hours; famous medieval collection.

Accommodation: All 1st and 3rd years housed in college, 2nd years in college-owned hostels and homes.

Facilities include: Sports ground; boathouse, etc.

Other features include: The college has more medical students than any other Cambridge college; music tradition – college orchestra; strong medical tradition.

Known as: Caius (pronounced *keys*)

Homerton College

Founded: 1976.

Students: 550 undergraduates; undergraduate male–female ratio: 1–3.

Position: Set in the south-east suburbs of Cambridge, about a mile from the city centre.

Buildings: Victorian buildings, with later additions set in substantial grounds. 1996 teaching block and library.

Library: Major education collection.
Accommodation: Available for all 1st years and some 2nd and 3rd years.
Facilities include: Sports ground and other sporting facilities on site; science laboratories, etc.
Other features include: This former teaching college still specialises in Edfucation Studies.

HUGHES HALL
Founded: 1885.
Students: 89 undergraduates; undergraduate male–female ratio: 3–1; admits mature undergraduates aged 21 and over and affiliated students.
Position: Overlooks university cricket ground, close to city sports hall and swimming pool; ten minutes' walk from city centre.
Buildings: Listed Victorian main building and modern additions.
Library: Learning Resources Centre (consisting of reading room and well-equipped computer room), open 24 hours.
Accommodation: Available for all three years.
Facilities include: Large garden and car parking facilities.
Other features include: This primarily graduate college has recently started to admit mature undergraduates.

JESUS COLLEGE
Founded: 1496.
Students: 503 undergraduates; undergraduate male–female ratio: 5–4.
Position: Situated in exceptionally spacious grounds, away from the tourist beat, yet only five minutes' walk from the city centre, the college offers a tranquil environment for living and working together with an unusually wide range of on-site facilities.
Buildings: Built around a 12th-century nunnery. Variety of buildings ranging from the Chapel which dates from about 1140 and is the oldest college building in Cambridge, to the Quincentenary Library and computing centre opened in 1996.

Library: Open 24 hours a day.

Accommodation: Provided for all undergraduates in their first three years of study.

Facilities include: Sports grounds, tennis and squash courts on site, boathouse close to college, computing centre, music practice rooms.

Other features include: Quiet situation, beautiful gardens; musical tradition. The only college with all its sports fields and facilities immediately surrounding it, it is known for its sporting tradition, especially in rugby.

KING'S COLLEGE

Founded: 1441.

Students: 383 undergraduates; undergraduate male–female ratio: 5–4.

Position: Prime position on either side of the Cam.

Buildings: Its magnificent buildings, in particular the dominating Chapel – perhaps the finest Perpendicular structure in England – are to many people the best known in Cambridge.

Library: Very large library open until midnight; special music collection.

Accommodation: Available to all undergraduates.

Facilities include: Sports ground; tennis and squash courts nearby; punts, boathouse, etc.

Other features include: Outstanding music tradition – world-famous choir, two orchestras. Known for good ents.

LUCY CAVENDISH COLLEGE

Founded: 1965.

Students: 135 undergraduates; all women; admits mature undergraduates aged 21 and over and affiliated students.

Position: In easy walking distance of city centre.

Buildings: Victorian and modern.

Library: Open 24 hours a day.

Accommodation: Available for all students; all en suite.

Facilities include: Computer room; exercise room.

Other features include: This is a unique college for mature women students, aged 21 or over.

MAGDALENE COLLEGE

Founded: 1428.

Students: 345 undergraduates; undergraduate male–female ratio: 1–1.

Position: Perfect position off the mainstream tourist route but enjoying the longest river frontage of any college right in the heart of the city.

Buildings: Charming architecture of a 'domestic' nature, ranging from 16th- and 17th-century 'cottages' to more recent additions.

Library: Four libraries, open until midnight. Two for undergraduates, one for Law.

Accommodation: Available to all undergraduates.

Facilities include: Sports ground – shared with St John's; squash courts; music room, darkroom and multigym.

Other features include: Magdalene (pronounced *maudlin*) retains a number of traditions abandoned by the rest of the university, including candle-lit Formal Hall.

NEW HALL

Founded: 1954.

Students: 360 undergraduates; all female.

Position: Half a mile north of the city centre.

Buildings: Built largely in the 1960s, major extensions have been recently completed.

Library: 24-hour access.

Accommodation: Available to all. 112 new rooms with en suite facilities.

Facilities include: Computing, music rooms, art room, darkroom, squash court, tennis courts.

Other features include: Modern, well-equipped buildings; contemporary art collection. Features a dining room that rises out of the floor!

NEWNHAM COLLEGE

Founded: 1871.

Students: 401 undergraduates; all female.

Position: In the west of the city, opposite the main arts faculties.

Buildings: A mixture of elegant Victorian architecture and pleasant modern buildings.

Library: Open until midnight.
Accommodation: Available to all undergraduates.
Facilities include: Tennis courts; sports ground; multi-gym; music and computer room.
Other features include: Spacious attractive gardens.

PEMBROKE COLLEGE
Founded: 1347.
Students: 400 undergraduates; undergraduate male–female ratio: 1–1.
Position: Close to town centre.
Buildings: An attractive range of buildings including medieval, 17th century and Victorian, and including a notable chapel by Wren.
Library: Open until midnight.
Accommodation: Available to all undergraduates, in college and college houses.
Facilities include: Computer and word-processing room; sports ground; tennis and squash courts; boat-house.
Other features include: Particularly pleasant garden.

PETERHOUSE
Founded: 1284.
Students: 284 undergraduates; undergraduate male–female ratio: 2–1.
Position: South of city centre.
Buildings: Particularly picturesque buildings dating from every century since the 13th.
Library: New large library, separate Law library.
Accommodation: Available for all undergraduates for three or four years.
Facilities include: Squash court; sports ground.
Other features include: Theatre converted from Victorian lecture hall. Peterhouse is the smallest of the medieval foundations in Cambridge.

QUEENS' COLLEGE
Founded: 1448.
Students: 490 undergraduates; undergraduate male–female ratio: 3–2.

Position: On either side of the Cam in the centre of the city.

Buildings: Fine range of medieval buildings including the wellknown half-timbered Cloister Court.

Library: Open until 1am – recently renovated and refurbished within a medieval chapel.

Accommodation: Available to all undergraduates – showers near all rooms.

Facilities include: Sports ground; modern boathouse, theatre; multigym.

Other features include: Particularly attractive riverside site; excellent dining facilities. Known for good ents.

ROBINSON COLLEGE

Founded: 1981.

Students: 397 undergraduates; undergraduate male–female ratio: 3–2.

Position: In the west of the city, well placed for most faculties.

Buildings: Dramatic brick 'castle' on wooded ground beside a stream dammed to form a pond within land-scaped gardens.

Library: Open until midnight; separate Law library.

Accommodation: Available to all undergraduates.

Facilities include: Shared sports facilities including sports ground, boathouse, etc; large auditorium.

Other features include: The only college in Cambridge founded for male and female students, graduates and undergraduates.

ST CATHARINE'S COLLEGE

Founded: 1473.

Students: 436 undergraduates; undergraduate male–female ratio: 1–1.

Position: Compact site very centrally placed; plus a new court at St Chad's by the University Library.

Buildings: An interesting mix of 17th- and 18th-century buildings with lively 20th-century additions.

Library: New and Old Libraries, both open 24 hours.

Accommodation: Available for all three years.

Facilities include: Tennis, badminton and squash courts; sports ground; boathouse.

Other features include: Good percentage of intake from the state sector.

Known as: Catz.

St Edmund's College

Founded: 1896.

Students: 110 undergraduates; undergraduate male–female ratio: 5–4; admits mature undergraduates aged 21 and over and affiliated students.

Position: Near the University Library and Science departments in west Cambridge site.

Buildings: Substantial extended 19th-century building set in extensive grounds with recent additions.

Library: Open 24 hours.

Accommodation: For many single and some married students.

Facilities include: Soccer pitch and tennis court within grounds, otherwise sports facilities shared with other colleges. Rowing, rugby.

Other features include: Though primarily a graduate college, a number of mature (ie those who are at least 21 years of age) undergraduates and affiliated students are admitted (refer to the college); Roman Catholic chapel providing for members of all Christian churches and other world religions.

St John's College

Founded: 1511.

Students: 550 undergraduates; undergraduate male–female ratio: 3–2.

Position: Central position on either side of the Cam.

Buildings: One of the largest colleges, St John's is also one of the most beautiful in its riverside setting and in the architecture of its buildings which date from the Tudor period to the present day.

Library: Open 24 hours.

Accommodation: Available to all undergraduates.

Facilities include: Large sports ground; boathouse; tennis and squash courts; multigym; theatre; arts studio; music practice rooms; computer room.

Other features include: A particularly well-endowed college with facilities to match; over 120 Fellows; strong in sports and music; world-famous choir.

SELWYN COLLEGE
Founded: 1882.
Students: 350 undergraduates; undergraduate male–female ratio: 5–4.
Position: Across the Cam, near to the University Library and Arts faculties.
Buildings: Victorian Gothic of a particularly attractive appearance, together with some modern architecture, eg in Cripps Court.
Library: Open until 2am.
Accommodation: Available to all undergraduates.
Facilities include: Sports ground shared with King's; boathouse.
Other features include: Pleasant garden; all major sports facilities on one site near college.

SIDNEY SUSSEX COLLEGE
Founded: 1596.
Students: 340 undergraduates; undergraduate male–female ratio: 1–1.
Position: Prime site right in the city centre.
Buildings: Impressive 16th- and 17th-century architecture in two courts plus a modern addition, Cromwell Court, side by side with attractive gardens.
Library: Open 24 hours.
Accommodation: Available to all undergraduates for three years.
Facilities include: Squash court; boathouse; sports ground about a mile away.
Other features include: College is strong in facilities for music; usually raises more money than any other college in Rag Week.
Known as: Sidney.

TRINITY COLLEGE
Founded: 1546.

Students: 663 undergraduates; undergraduate male–female ratio: 3–2.

Position: The largest college, centrally placed on either side of the Cam.

Buildings: Contains some of the finest architecture in the university including 16th-century Great Court, the largest in Cambridge, or Oxford for that matter, and 17th-century Nevile's Court with the glorious Wren library.

Library: Largest college library in Cambridge; open until midnight most days; almost all student requests are purchased.

Accommodation: Available to all undergraduates.

Facilities include: Three sports grounds; tennis and squash courts; boathouse; theatre.

Other features include: Strong science and mathematics tradition – the college founded Britain's first science park on the outskirts of the city; well endowed so offers very good financial assistance packages.

TRINITY HALL
Founded: 1350.

Students: 359 undergraduates; undergraduate male–female ratio: 3–2.

Position: Close-knit compact central site, with new residential buildings nearby and by the sports fields.

Buildings: Beautiful mix of historic buildings, some in mellow brick, eg the lovely 17th-century library.

Library: Open 24 hours; separate Law library.

Accommodation: Available to all undergraduates for three years.

Facilities include: Theatre; sports ground; boathouse; music room; computer room.

Other features include: Traditions of success in music, drama and sport; strong Law tradition.

Known as: Tit Hall.

WOLFSON COLLEGE
Founded: 1965.
Students: 90 undergraduates; undergraduate male–female ratio: 5–4; admits mature undergraduates aged 21 and over and affiliated students.
Position: In west of the city close to the university library.
Buildings: Mostly modern (1970s, 1995) low-rise buildings set around courts with large gardens adjoining. All rooms have computer sockets, about half have telephone sockets, and around 60% have own shower and toilet.
Library: Access 24 hours a day.
Accommodation: Available on site to all Wolfson students.
Facilities include: Sports and music facilities; large computer network; attractive grounds.
Other features include: This primarily graduate college also admits mature and affiliated undergraduates (over 21 years old). Applicants should write to the Admissions Tutor.

CAMBRIDGE GRADUATE COLLEGES

The following colleges do not admit undergraduates:

■ Clare Hall
■ Darwin.

OXFORD UNDER- GRADUATE NUMBERS BY SUBJECT

The figures below give the total number of under- graduates for the 2005–6 academic year.

ARCHAEOLOGY & ANTHROPOLOGY

Harris Manchester	5	St Hilda's	5
Hertford	7	St Hugh's	17
Keble	17	St John's	7
Magdalen	5	St Peter's	11
New College	1	Wadham	1

BIOCHEMISTRY

Balliol	7	Pembroke	16
Brasenose	15	Queen's	15
Christ Church	13	St Anne's	14
Corpus Christi	14	St Catherine's	16
Exeter	19	St Edmund Hall	10
Hertford	10	St Hilda's	15
Jesus	8	St Hugh's	14
Lady Margaret Hall	11	St John's	9
Lincoln	9	St Peter's	14
Magdalen	8	Somerville	15
Merton	16	Trinity	20
New College	14	University College	14
Oriel	17	Wadham	14

BIOLOGICAL SCIENCES

Balliol	9	Queen's	13
Brasenose	13	St Anne's	11
Christ Church	19	St Catherine's	21
Hertford	10	St Hilda's	21
Jesus	6	St Hugh's	18
Keble	12	St John's	11
Lady Margaret Hall	11	St Peter's	13
Magdalen	15	Somerville	13
Merton	11	University College	1
New College	11	Wadham	17
Pembroke	21	Worcester	13

CHEMISTRY

Balliol	32	Queen's	15
Brasenose	23	St Anne's	13
Christ Church	24	St Catherine's	38
Corpus Christi	13	St Edmund Hall	20
Exeter	22	St Hilda's	21
Hertford	15	St Hugh's	23
Jesus	27	St John's	34
Keble	30	St Peter's	13
Lady Margaret Hall	18	Somerville	23
Lincoln	12	Trinity	17
Magdalen	24	University College	45
Merton	24	Wadham	31
New College	30	Worcester	23
Oriel	15	Wycliffe Hall	1
Pembroke	28		

CLASSICAL ARCHAEOLOGY AND ANCIENT HISTORY

Balliol	6	New College	2
Christ Church	3	Oriel	2
Corpus Christi	2	Regent's Park	1
Exeter	2	St Hilda's	2
Keble	5	St John's	5
Lady Margaret Hall	5	Somerville	4
Magdalen	5	Wadham	3
Merton	2	Worcester	2

CLASSICS

Balliol	30	Queen's	15
Brasenose	24	St Anne's	17
Christ Church	20	St Benet's Hall	6
Corpus Christi	29	St Hilda's	26
Exeter	17	St Hugh's	17
Jesus	14	St John's	17
Keble	7	Somerville	18
Lady Margaret Hall	20	Trinity	24
Magdalen	25	University College	19
Merton	19	Wadham	25
New College	22	Worcester	17
Oriel	17		

CLASSICS AND ENGLISH

Brasenose	1	St Anne's	3
Corpus Christi	5	St Hilda's	1
Jesus	1	St Hugh's	1
Lady Margaret Hall	6	St John's	1
Magdalen	1	Somerville	1
Merton	1	University College	1
Oriel	2	Wadham	2
Queen's	3	Worcester	2

CLASSICS AND MODERN LANGUAGES

Balliol	1	St Anne's	2
Brasenose	11	St Hilda's	1
Christ Church	4	St Hugh's	2
Exeter	3	St John's	2
Keble	3	Somerville	1
Magdalen	5	Trinity	1
New College	4	University College	3
Oriel	1	Wadham	2
Queen's	3	Worcester	3

COMPUTER SCIENCE

Balliol	6	St Anne's	3
Brasenose	1	St Catherine's	8
Hertford	2	St Edmund Hall	6
Keble	8	St Hugh's	1
Lady Margaret Hall	5	St John's	2
Lincoln	7		
Magdalen	3	Somerville	3
Merton	3	University College	5
New College	4	Wadham	3
Oriel	6	Worcester	7

EARTH SCIENCES

Exeter	11	St Hugh's	2
Hertford	13	St Peter's	12
Jesus	7	University College	15
St Anne's	12	Worcester	14
St Edmund Hall	27		

ECONOMICS AND MANAGEMENT

Balliol	10	Pembroke	23
Brasenose	17	Queen's	10
Christ Church	8	St Anne's	13
Corpus Christi	4	St Catherine's	6
Exeter	11	St Edmund Hall	13
Harris Manchester	3	St Hilda's	10
Hertford	23	St Hugh's	10
Jesus	11	St John's	3
Keble	13	St Peter's	15
Lady Margaret Hall	8	Trinity	8
Lincoln	7	University College	7
Merton	11	Wadham	9
New College	7	Worcester	8

ENGINEERING SCIENCE

Balliol	21	Pembroke	23
Brasenose	17	Queen's	8
Christ Church	20	St Anne's	17
Corpus Christi	6	St Catherine's	26
Exeter	19	St Edmund Hall	26
Hertford	16	St Hilda's	7
Jesus	11	St Hugh's	19
Keble	28	St John's	22
Lady Margaret Hall	22	St Peter's	5
Lincoln	15	Somerville	18
Magdalen	17	Trinity	9
Mansfield	9	University College	25
New College	14	Wadham	20
Oriel	18	Worcester	18

ENGINEERING AND COMPUTING SCIENCE

Balliol	2	St Anne's	2
Brasenose	2	St Edmund Hall	1
Exeter	2	St Hilda's	1
Hertford	1	St Hugh's	2
Jesus	1	St John's	3
Keble	1	Somerville	2
Lady Margaret Hall	1	Trinity	1
Magdalen	1	University College	3
Oriel	4	Worcester	1
Pembroke	2		

ENGINEERING, ECONOMICS AND MANAGEMENT

Balliol	12	Queen's	1
Brasenose	2	St Anne's	2
Christ Church	3	St Catherine's	5
Exeter	1	St Edmund Hall	4
Hertford	3	St Hilda's	5
Jesus	5	St Hugh's	2
Keble	9	St Peter's	2
Lincoln	4	Somerville	3
Magdalen	3	Trinity	3
Mansfield	4	University College	1
New College	10	Wadham	5
Pembroke	2		

ENGINEERING AND MATERIALS

Brasenose	1	St Hilda's	1
Corpus Christi	1	Trinity	2

ENGLISH

Balliol	26	Oriel	14
Brasenose	22	Pembroke	31
Christ Church	30	Regent's Park	16
Corpus Christi	17	St Anne's	41
Exeter	23	St Benet's Hall	4
Greyfriars	12	St Catherine's	22
Harris Manchester	16	St Edmund Hall	31
Hertford	25	St Hilda's	34
Jesus	19	St Hugh's	30
Keble	30	St John's	21
Lady Margaret Hall	37	St Peter's	27
Lincoln	28	Somerville	36
Magdalen	19	Trinity	21
Mansfield	20	University College	26
Merton	16	Wadham	32
New College	24	Worcester	21

ENGLISH AND MODERN LANGUAGES

College		College	
Balliol	1	St Anne's	1
Brasenose	2	St Catherine's	1
Exeter	2	St Edmund Hall	3
Harris Manchester	1	St Hilda's	4
Jesus	4	St Hugh's	3
Lady Margaret Hall	2	St John's	1
Lincoln	1	St Peter's	4
Magdalen	2	Somerville	1
Merton	2	Trinity	3
New College	6	Wadham	12
Queen's	6	Worcester	1

ENGLISH AND MIDDLE EASTERN LANGUAGES

College		College	
Christ Church	1	St Catherine's	1
Jesus	1	St Hugh's	1
Magdalen	2	St John's	6
Merton	2	Somerville	1
Pembroke	3	Wadham	2
Queen's	1	Worcester	1
St Anne's	2		

EXPERIMENTAL PSYCHOLOGY

College		College	
Balliol	9	Pembroke	5
Brasenose	4	Queen's	8
Christ Church	8	St Anne's	8
Corpus Christi	6	St Catherine's	5
Greyfriars	1	St Edmund Hall	6
Harris Manchester	3	St Hilda's	10
Hertford	5	St Hugh's	5
Jesus	4	St John's	6
Lady Margaret Hall	5	Somerville	6
Magdalen	3	University College	7
New College	10	Wadham	7
Oriel	2	Worcester	4

FINE ART

Balliol	2	St Anne's	4
Brasenose	3	St Catherine's	5
Christ Church	3	St Edmund Hall	12
Exeter	3	St Hilda's	2
Hertford	1	St Hugh's	3
Lady Margaret Hall	4	St John's	2
Magdalen	2	University College	4
New College	1	Worcester	2
Pembroke	3		

GEOGRAPHY

Brasenose	14	St Catherine's	32
Christ Church	11	St Edmund Hall	22
Harris Manchester	2	St Hilda's	12
Hertford	33	St Hugh's	3
Mansfield	26	St John's	12
Merton	1	St Peter's	17
Regent's Park	8	Wadham	2
St Anne's	14	Worcester	12
St Benet's Hall	2		

HISTORY (ANCIENT AND MODERN)

Balliol	1	Queen's	3
Brasenose	5	St Anne's	1
Christ Church	4	St Benet's Hall	1
Corpus Christi	5	St Hilda's	7
Greyfriars	1	St Hugh's	5
Keble	1	St John's	5
Lady Margaret Hall	2	St Peter's	1
Lincoln	1	Somerville	4
Magdalen	4	Trinity	2
Merton	2	University College	4
New College	2	Wadham	1
Oriel	1	Worcester	4

HISTORY (MODERN)

Balliol	38	Pembroke	21
Brasenose	27	Queen's	15
Christ Church	36	Regent's Park	8
Corpus Christi	12	St Anne's	25
Exeter	25	St Benet's Hall	10
Greyfriars	9	St Catherine's	28
Harris Manchester	3	St Edmund Hall	25
Hertford	23	St Hilda's	21
Jesus	18	St Hugh's	30
Keble	23	St John's	19
Lady Margaret Hall	29	St Peter's	25
Lincoln	28	Somerville	32
Magdalen	36	Trinity	18
Mansfield	18	University College	35
Merton	24	Wadham	24
New College	26	Worcester	28
Oriel	24		

HISTORY (MODERN) AND ECONOMICS

Balliol	1	Pembroke	10
Corpus Christi	1	St Anne's	1
Hertford	3	St John's	4
Merton	2	Somerville	1
New College	1		

HISTORY (MODERN) AND ENGLISH

Balliol	2	Merton	4
Corpus Christi	1	Pembroke	1
Exeter	2	Regent's Park	1
Greyfriars	3	St Catherine's	2
Harris Manchester	2	St Hugh's	1
Hertford	1	St John's	1
Jesus	5	St Peter's	1
Keble	1	Wadham	6
Lincoln	1	Worcester	2
Mansfield	5		

HISTORY (MODERN) AND MODERN LANGUAGES

Balliol	4	St Anne's	1
Brasenose	2	St Catherine's	2
Christ Church	1	St Edmund Hall	2
Exeter	1	St Hilda's	3
Hertford	10	St Hugh's	4
Jesus	3	St John's	5
Keble	1	St Peter's	1
Lincoln	18	Somerville	3
Magdalen	3	Trinity	3
Merton	4	University College	3
New College	5	Wadham	5
Pembroke	5	Worcester	5
Queen's	1		

HISTORY (MODERN) AND POLITICS

Balliol	11	Oriel	1
Brasenose	4	Pembroke	8
Christ Church	9	Queen's	17
Corpus Christi	6	St Anne's	3
Exeter	1	St Benet's Hall	3
Greyfriars	1	St Catherine's	5
Hertford	2	St Edmund Hall	4
Jesus	5	St Hilda's	7
Keble	3	St Hugh's	2
Lady Margaret Hall	9	St John's	4
Lincoln	5	St Peter's	6
Magdalen	9	Trinity	2
Mansfield	6	University College	3
Merton	10	Wadham	7
New College	4	Worcester	3

HISTORY OF ART

Christ Church	4	St Peter's	4
Harris Manchester	1	Wadham	5
St Catherine's	5	Worcester	2

HUMAN SCIENCES

Harris Manchester	4	Regent's Park	2
Hertford	8	St Anne's	3
Jesus	6	St Catherine's	17
Keble	1	St Hilda's	5
Lady Margaret Hall	9	St Hugh's	9
Magdalen	9	St John's	9
Mansfield	6	St Peter's	1
New College	11	Somerville	10
Pembroke	1	Wadham	6

LAW

Balliol	23	Oriel	28
Brasenose	31	Pembroke	25
Campion Hall	1	Queen's	15
Christ Church	31	Regent's Park	5
Corpus Christi	21	St Anne's	21
Exeter	27	St Benet's Hall	2
Greyfriars	7	St Catherine's	27
Harris Manchester	15	St Edmund Hall	26
Hertford	22	St Hilda's	24
Jesus	26	St Hugh's	24
Keble	31	St John's	23
Lady Margaret Hall	30	St Peter's	15
Lincoln	32	Somerville	19
Magdalen	26	Trinity	20
Mansfield	13	University College	32
Merton	23	Wadham	34
New College	24	Worcester	32

MATERIALS, ECONOMICS AND MANAGEMENT

Mansfield	3	St Edmund Hall	4
St Anne's	3	Trinity	5

MATERIALS SCIENCE

Corpus Christi	10	St Catherine's	16
Mansfield	9	St Edmund Hall	8
Queen's	6	Trinity	18
St Anne's	14		

MATHEMATICS

Balliol	23	Pembroke	23
Brasenose	19	Queen's	25
Christ Church	18	St Anne's	22
Corpus Christi	17	St Catherine's	22
Exeter	25	St Edmund Hall	10
Hertford	17	St Hilda's	18
Jesus	27	St Hugh's	28
Keble	15	St John's	27
Lady Margaret Hall	27	St Peter's	19
Lincoln	18	Somerville	21
Magdalen	15	Trinity	17
Mansfield	18	University College	22
Merton	20	Wadham	34
New College	19	Worcester	23
Oriel	20		

MATHEMATICS AND COMPUTER SCIENCE

Balliol	3	Queen's	1
Corpus Christi	1	St Anne's	4
Exeter	1	St Catherine's	4
Hertford	2	St Edmund Hall	2
Keble	6	St Hugh's	3
Lady Margaret Hall	6	St John's	1
Lincoln	2	Trinity	1
Magdalen	3	University College	2
Merton	3	Wadham	2
New College	3	Worcester	5
Oriel	1		

MATHEMATICS AND PHILOSOPHY

Balliol	9	Queen's	1
Brasenose	1	St Anne's	2
Christ Church	4	St Catherine's	2
Corpus Christi	2	St Edmund Hall	4
Exeter	7	St Hilda's	4
Jesus	2	St Hugh's	5
Keble	1	St John's	3
Lady Margaret Hall	2	St Peter's	6
Magdalen	5	Somerville	2
Mansfield	3	Trinity	1
Merton	6	University College	3
New College	5	Wadham	3
Pembroke	6	Worcester	8

MATHEMATICS AND STATISTICS

Brasenose	1	St Anne's	4
Christ Church	1	St Catherine's	4
Corpus Christi	3	St Hilda's	10
Exeter	3	St Hugh's	6
Keble	5	St John's	1
Lady Margaret Hall	9	St Peter's	7
Lincoln	6	Somerville	6
Magdalen	1	Trinity	1
Mansfield	3	Wadham	1
Merton	3	Worcester	11
Queen's	3		

MODERN LANGUAGES

Balliol	12	Regent's Park	1
Brasenose	14	St Anne's	30
Christ Church	31	St Catherine's	27
Exeter	20	St Edmund Hall	24
Hertford	18	St Hilda's	33
Jesus	14	St Hugh's	24
Keble	22	St John's	18
Lady Margaret Hall	28	St Peter's	21
Magdalen	15	Somerville	21
Merton	12	Trinity	13
New College	26	University College	10
Oriel	23	Wadham	20
Pembroke	26	Worcester	16
Queen's	30		

MUSIC

Brasenose	4	Pembroke	6
Christ Church	17	Queen's	9
Corpus Christi	2	St Anne's	6
Exeter	5	St Catherine's	11
Hertford	6	St Edmund Hall	4
Jesus	6	St Hilda's	5
Keble	3	St Hugh's	5
Lady Margaret Hall	7	St John's	2
Lincoln	4	St Peter's	10
Magdalen	14	Somerville	7
Merton	5	Trinity	1
New College	15	University College	3
Oriel	4	Worcester	12

ORIENTAL STUDIES

Balliol	2	Pembroke	37
Christ Church	3	Queen's	13
Corpus Christi	1	St Anne's	14
Exeter	1	St Catherine's	5
Greyfriars	1	St Hilda's	13
Harris Manchester	6	St Hugh's	2
Hertford	19	St John's	5
Keble	5	Somerville	5
Magdalen	1	University College	7
Mansfield	4	Wadham	29
New College	1	Worcester	2

PHILOSOPHY AND MODERN LANGUAGES

Balliol	1	St Anne's	2
Brasenose	6	St Catherine's	1
Christ Church	2	St Edmund Hall	2
Exeter	8	St Hilda's	4
Lady Margaret Hall	2	St John's	3
Lincoln	2	St Peter's	3
Magdalen	2	Somerville	4
New College	6	Trinity	1
Oriel	1	University College	1
Pembroke	1	Wadham	6
Queen's	2	Worcester	2

PHILOSOPHY, POLITICS AND ECONOMICS

Balliol	44	Pembroke	30
Brasenose	31	Queen's	25
Christ Church	30	Regent's Park	9
Corpus Christi	18	St Anne's	27
Exeter	19	St Benet's Hall	5
Greyfriars	1	St Catherine's	20
Harris Manchester	20	St Edmund Hall	29
Hertford	19	St Hilda's	25
Jesus	20	St Hugh's	22
Keble	28	St John's	20
Lady Margaret Hall	22	St Peter's	32
Lincoln	29	Somerville	31
Magdalen	33	Trinity	17
Mansfield	20	University College	28
Merton	26	Wadham	31
New College	37	Worcester	19
Oriel	23		

PHILOSOPHY AND THEOLOGY

Blackfriars	1	Queen's	2
Christ Church	3	Regent's Park	9
Harris Manchester	2	St Benet's Hall	2
Jesus	3	St Hilda's	2
Keble	7	St John's	4
Lady Margaret Hall	3	St Peter's	6
Mansfield	2	Trinity	6
Oriel	10	Worcester	5
Pembroke	4	Wycliffe Hall	2

PHYSICS

Balliol	22	Oriel	19
Brasenose	18	Queen's	21
Christ Church	21	St Anne's	20
Corpus Christi	19	St Catherine's	27
Exeter	17	St Edmund Hall	29
Hertford	28	St Hilda's	13
Jesus	27	St Hugh's	19
Keble	35	St John's	24
Lady Margaret Hall	19	St Peter's	17
Lincoln	20	Somerville	19
Magdalen	20	Trinity	19
Mansfield	24	University College	28
Merton	29	Wadham	27
New College	18	Worcester	22

PHYSICS AND PHILOSOPHY

Balliol	14	St Anne's	2
Brasenose	3	St Edmund Hall	4
Christ Church	1	St Hilda's	3
Exeter	9	St Peter's	3
Hertford	2	Somerville	3
Lady Margaret Hall	1	Trinity	3
Magdalen	1	University College	2
New College	3	Wadham	1
Oriel	3	Worcester	1
Queen's	1		

PHYSIOLOGICAL SCIENCES

Balliol	4	New College	3
Brasenose	1	Queen's	2
Corpus Christi	2	St Catherine's	4
Exeter	4	St Hilda's	1
Hertford	4	St Hugh's	1
Keble	6	St Peter's	2
Lady Margaret Hall	4	Somerville	1
Lincoln	3	University College	6
Magdalen	5	Wadham	1

PRE-CLINICAL MEDICINE

Balliol	12	Pembroke	13
Brasenose	24	Queen's	18
Christ Church	16	St Anne's	24
Corpus Christi	13	St Catherine's	14
Exeter	17	St Edmund Hall	12
Hertford	14	St Hilda's	18
Jesus	11	St Hugh's	19
Keble	17	St John's	17
Lady Margaret Hall	16	St Peter's	16
Lincoln	16	Somerville	17
Magdalen	16	Trinity	19
Merton	16	University College	12
New College	16	Wadham	15
Oriel	18	Worcester	18

PSYCHOLOGY, PHILOSOPHY AND PHYSIOLOGY

Balliol	7	Queen's	4
Brasenose	7	St Anne's	4
Christ Church	3	St Catherine's	3
Corpus Christi	5	St Edmund Hall	7
Harris Manchester	6	St Hilda's	11
Hertford	3	St Hugh's	5
Jesus	3	St John's	6
Lady Margaret Hall	2	Somerville	8
Magdalen	10	University College	8
New College	6	Wadham	4
Oriel	5	Worcester	5
Pembroke	7		

THEOLOGY

Balliol	1	Pembroke	10
Blackfriars	1	Regent's Park	20
Christ Church	5	St Benet's Hall	11
Corpus Christi	1	St Hilda's	3
Harris Manchester	7	St John's	7
Greyfriars	5	St Peter's	9
Keble	10	St Stephen's House	1
Lady Margaret Hall	9	Trinity	5
Mansfield	12	Worcester	15
Oriel	3	Wycliffe Hall	25

CAMBRIDGE UNDER-GRADUATE NUMBERS BY SUBJECT

The figures below give the number of first-year undergraduates admitted in 2005.

ANGLO-SAXON, NORSE AND CELTIC

Christ's	1	Newnham	2
Clare	1	Pembroke	3
Corpus Christi	1	Peterhouse	1
Downing	1	Queens'	1
Fitzwilliam	1	Robinson	1
Girton	3	St Catharine's	2
Gonville and Caius	1	St John's	1
Homerton	1	Selwyn	1
Hughes Hall	1	Trinity	2

ARCHITECTURE

Churchill	4	New Hall	1
Clare	3	Newnham	2
Downing	2	Pembroke	2
Emmanuel	1	Queens'	1
Fitzwilliam	1	Robinson	2
Girton	2	St John's	3
Jesus	1	Selwyn	1
King's	1	Sidney Sussex	1
Lucy Cavendish	1	Trinity	2
Magdalene	4	Trinity Hall	2

ARCHAEOLOGY AND ANTHROPOLOGY

Christ's	2	King's	4
Churchill	5	Lucy Cavendish	1
Clare	1	Magdalene	2
Corpus Christi	4	New Hall	5
Downing	3	Newnham	3
Emmanuel	2	Pembroke	2
Fitzwilliam	2	Robinson	2
Girton	6	St Catharine's	2
Gonville and Caius	2	St John's	2
Homerton	7	Selwyn	2
Hughes Hall	2	Trinity	2
Jesus	2	Trinity Hall	1

CLASSICS

Christ's	3	New Hall	1
Churchill	5	Newnham	5
Clare	4	Pembroke	5
Corpus Christi	3	Peterhouse	4
Downing	4	Queens'	2
Emmanuel	2	Robinson	3
Fitzwilliam	2	St Catharine's	1
Girton	4	St John's	5
Gonville and Caius	2	Selwyn	2
Jesus	2	Sidney Sussex	3
King's	7	Trinity	4
Lucy Cavendish	1	Trinity Hall	3
Magdalene	2		

CLASSICS (FOUR YEARS)

Gonville and Caius	1	New Hall	2
Jesus	1	Robinson	1
King's	2		

COMPUTER SCIENCE

Christ's	2	Pembroke	3
Churchill	10	Peterhouse	1
Clare	2	Queens'	5
Corpus Christi	1	Robinson	6
Fitzwilliam	6	St Catharine's	2
Girton	2	St John's	2
Gonville and Caius	6	Selwyn	1
Homerton	3	Sidney Sussex	1
Jesus	6	Trinity	2
King's	2	Trinity Hall	2
Newnham	1		

ECONOMICS

Christ's	6	New Hall	2
Churchill	6	Newnham	6
Clare	4	Pembroke	4
Corpus Christi	3	Peterhouse	3
Downing	7	Queens'	6
Emmanuel	3	Robinson	4
Fitzwilliam	9	St Catharine's	9
Girton	8	St Edmund's	6
Gonville and Caius	10	St John's	11
Homerton	4	Selwyn	4
Hughes Hall	5	Sidney Sussex	8
Jesus	5	Trinity	11
King's	7	Trinity Hall	5
Magdalene	4	Wolfson	2

EDUCATION

Christ's	2	Queens'	1
Churchill	1	St John's	1
Homerton	72	Wolfson	1
Jesus	1		

ENGINEERING

Christ's	12	New Hall	8
Churchill	16	Newnham	4
Clare	8	Pembroke	16
Corpus Christi	2	Peterhouse	7
Downing	12	Queens'	17
Emmanuel	19	Robinson	11
Fitzwilliam	13	St Catharine's	7
Girton	12	St Edmund's	1
Gonville and Caius	12	St John's	19
Homerton	12	Selwyn	11
Jesus	14	Sidney Sussex	9
King's	8	Trinity	20
Magdalene	13	Trinity Hall	5

ENGLISH

Christ's	6	Magdalene	6
Churchill	6	New Hall	8
Clare	10	Newnham	7
Corpus Christi	8	Pembroke	10
Downing	6	Peterhouse	7
Emmanuel	8	Queens'	9
Fitzwilliam	6	Robinson	7
Girton	10	St Catharine's	10
Gonville and Caius	10	St John's	8
Homerton	9	Selwyn	6
Hughes Hall	2	Sidney Sussex	7
Jesus	11	Trinity	13
King's	6	Trinity Hall	7
Lucy Cavendish	3	Wolfson	2

GEOGRAPHY

Christ's	5	Magdalene	2
Churchill	5	Newnham	7
Clare	2	Queens'	2
Corpus Christi	2	Robinson	6
Downing	5	St Catharine's	7
Emmanuel	8	St Edmund's	3
Fitzwilliam	7	St John's	7
Girton	7	Selwyn	1
Homerton	3	Sidney Sussex	5
Jesus	5	Trinity	1
King's	1	Trinity Hall	3

HISTORY

Christ's	10	Magdalene	6
Churchill	3	New Hall	10
Clare	11	Newnham	11
Corpus Christi	5	Pembroke	10
Downing	6	Peterhouse	13
Emmanuel	9	Queens'	9
Fitzwilliam	8	Robinson	6
Girton	9	St Catharine's	6
Gonville and Caius	14	St John's	6
Homerton	11	Selwyn	8
Hughes Hall	1	Sidney Sussex	9
Jesus	7	Trinity	7
King's	10	Trinity Hall	9
Lucy Cavendish	1		

HISTORY OF ART

Christ's	1	New Hall	1
Clare	1	Newnham	1
Downing	2	Pembroke	3
Emmanuel	2	Peterhouse	1
Fitzwilliam	1	Queens'	1
Girton	1	Robinson	1
Gonville and Caius	2	St John's	1
Homerton	3	Selwyn	1
Jesus	2	Trinity	3
King's	3	Trinity Hall	2
Magdalene	2	Wolfson	1

LAND ECONOMY

Christ's	1	Pembroke	2
Clare	1	Queens'	3
Downing	2	Robinson	5
Fitzwilliam	4	St Catharine's	4
Gonville and Caius	2	St Edmund's	3
Homerton	3	St John's	2
Hughes Hall	1	Selwyn	1
Jesus	2	Sidney Sussex	1
Magdalene	2	Trinity	2
Newnham	2	Trinity Hall	1

LAW

Christ's	3	New Hall	9
Churchill	5	Newnham	10
Clare	4	Pembroke	6
Corpus Christi	4	Peterhouse	8
Downing	17	Queens'	10
Emmanuel	6	Robinson	9
Fitzwilliam	6	St Catharine's	8
Girton	11	St Edmund's	4
Gonville and Caius	10	St John's	13
Homerton	7	Selwyn	9
Hughes Hall	4	Sidney Sussex	5
Jesus	10	Trinity	11
King's	1	Trinity Hall	9
Lucy Cavendish	2	Wolfson	3
Magdalene	8		

MATHEMATICS

Christ's	11	New Hall	5
Churchill	15	Newnham	4
Clare	7	Pembroke	9
Corpus Christi	3	Peterhouse	6
Downing	5	Queens'	16
Emmanuel	14	Robinson	9
Fitzwilliam	8	St Catharine's	8
Girton	13	St Edmund's	1
Gonville and Caius	11	St John's	17
Hughes Hall	1	Selwyn	6
Jesus	14	Sidney Sussex	7
King's	7	Trinity	39
Magdalene	7	Trinity Hall	7

MEDICINE

Christ's	13	Newnham	11
Churchill	11	Pembroke	8
Clare	12	Peterhouse	8
Corpus Christi	4	Queens'	13
Downing	17	Robinson	9
Emmanuel	18	St Catharine's	11
Fitzwilliam	10	St Edmund's	3
Girton	13	St John's	17
Gonville and Caius	23	Selwyn	10
Jesus	11	Sidney Sussex	11
King's	9	Trinity	14
Lucy Cavendish	1	Trinity Hall	10
Magdalene	9	Wolfson	2
New Hall	10		

MODERN AND MEDIEVAL LANGUAGES

Christ's	8	Magdalene	4
Churchill	4	New Hall	6
Clare	13	Newnham	8
Corpus Christi	2	Pembroke	7
Downing	4	Peterhouse	3
Emmanuel	7	Queens'	7
Fitzwilliam	6	Robinson	6
Girton	7	St Catharine's	11
Gonville and Caius	8	St John's	9
Homerton	5	Selwyn	10
Jesus	9	Sidney Sussex	5
King's	10	Trinity	11
Lucy Cavendish	1	Trinity Hall	10

MUSIC

Christ's	4	Magdalene	2
Churchill	2	New Hall	2
Clare	4	Newnham	2
Corpus Christi	4	Pembroke	1
Emmanuel	3	Peterhouse	2
Fitzwilliam	1	Robinson	3
Girton	3	St Catharine's	2
Gonville and Caius	4	St John's	4
Homerton	5	Selwyn	5
Jesus	2	Sidney Sussex	2
King's	7	Trinity	5
Lucy Cavendish	1	Trinity Hall	1

NATURAL SCIENCES

Christ's	22	New Hall	25
Churchill	27	Newnham	23
Clare	36	Pembroke	24
Corpus Christi	12	Peterhouse	10
Downing	25	Queens'	27
Emmanuel	25	Robinson	16
Fitzwilliam	32	St Catharine's	22
Girton	29	St Edmund's	14
Gonville and Caius	28	St John's	26
Homerton	29	Selwyn	3
Hughes Hall	1	Sidney Sussex	30
Jesus	30	Trinity	32
King's	17	Trinity Hall	18
Lucy Cavendish	1	Wolfson	2
Magdalene	15		

ORIENTAL STUDIES

Churchill	1	Magdalene	1
Clare	4	Pembroke	2
Corpus Christi	2	Queens'	2
Downing	1	Robinson	1
Emmanuel	2	St Catharine's	1
Fitzwilliam	1	St John's	1
Gonville and Caius	1	Trinity	3
Homerton	5	Wolfson	1
King's	1		

PHILOSOPHY

College		College	
Christ's	2	Newnham	1
Churchill	2	Pembroke	3
Clare	1	Peterhouse	1
Corpus Christi	2	Queens'	2
Downing	1	Robinson	1
Emmanuel	1	St Catharine's	2
Fitzwilliam	4	St Edmund's	1
Girton	1	St John's	3
Gonville and Caius	2	Selwyn	2
Homerton	1	Sidney Sussex	1
Jesus	1	Trinity	3
King's	3	Trinity Hall	2
New Hall	2	Wolfson	1

SOCIAL AND POLITICAL SCIENCES

College		College	
Christ's	3	Magdalene	3
Churchill	3	New Hall	6
Clare	3	Newnham	4
Corpus Christi	2	Pembroke	2
Downing	3	Queens'	3
Emmanuel	8	Robinson	6
Fitzwilliam	5	St Catharine's	4
Girton	3	St Edmund's	1
Gonville and Caius	4	St John's	4
Homerton	4	Selwyn	5
Hughes Hall	2	Sidney Sussex	5
Jesus	6	Trinity	4
King's	10	Trinity Hall	3
Lucy Cavendish	2		

THEOLOGY AND RELIGIOUS STUDIES

College		College	
Christ's	2	New Hall	2
Clare	2	Newnham	2
Corpus Christi	2	Pembroke	2
Emmanuel	2	Peterhouse	2
Fitzwilliam	3	Queens'	2
Girton	2	Robinson	1
Gonville and Caius	3	St Catharine's	2
Homerton	4	St John's	3
Jesus	1	Selwyn	1
King's	4	Sidney Sussex	1
Lucy Cavendish	1	Trinity	4
Magdalene	3	Trinity Hall	2

VETERINARY MEDICINE

Christ's	1	Newnham	3
Churchill	2	Pembroke	3
Clare	3	Queens'	4
Downing	2	Robinson	6
Emmanuel	6	St Catharine's	6
Fitzwilliam	2	St Edmund's	5
Girton	8	St John's	3
Gonville and Caius	2	Selwyn	5
Jesus	3	Sidney Sussex	2
Lucy Cavendish	2	Trinity	1
Magdalene	3	Trinity Hall	1
New Hall	5	Wolfson	3

5

MAXIMISING YOUR CHANCES PRE-INTERVIEW

APPLICATIONS By mid-September at the latest you will have selected your university and your course, and you will have either selected your college of first preference or decided to submit an open application. Now it's time to complete your application forms and submit them to your referee.

You have to complete two applications – one for UCAS and one for the university. The special form for Oxford is called the Oxford Application Form and is obtainable from your school or the Oxford Colleges Admissions Office. The special form for Cambridge is called the Cambridge Application Form (CAF), again obtainable through schools or directly from the Cambridge Admissions Office (CAO). Both are also available online. All forms have to arrive at their destinations by 15 October, so it is vital that you give your referee sufficient time to complete the paperwork.

MUSIC AWARD NOMINATIONS
Note that there are different deadlines and forms if you are applying for Organ, Choral, Repetiteur and Instrumental Awards. Most application forms require an application before the usual 15 October deadline but see the individual prospectuses for further information.

The general procedures and advice governing completion of the UCAS application are available on the UCAS website or are dealt with in *How to Complete Your UCAS Application* (Trotman) and are not repeated here. The completion of the special university forms is straightforward provided you follow the instructions and read the prospectuses. The main element that cannot be delegated to 'automatic pilot' is the personal statement.

PERSONAL STATEMENTS

In very general terms, the personal statement is an opportunity for you to present your extracurricular CV, to highlight areas of special academic interest and perhaps to make a 'mission statement' about what your course can do for you and what you can bring to your course. *How to Complete Your UCAS Application* contains examples of good and bad personal statements for university applications in general.

TWO PERSONAL STATEMENTS?

However, when applying to Oxbridge, the personal statement does not have to be (and arguably should not be) the same for both the forms that you have to submit. On the one hand, the personal statement on the UCAS application has to speak to each of the universities to which you are applying. There may well be slight or even significant differences between the courses which will lead you to generalise your statement of special academic interests and your mission statements.

On the other hand, the Oxford and Cambridge forms give you the opportunity to focus directly on a particular university, a particular course and, unless you are making an open application, a particular college. Remember however, not to duplicate anything you have said in your UCAS application.

You may for instance wish to draw attention to specifics in the course content which have attracted you to it over and above the same course at other institutions. Do note though that this section on the form is not an appropriate forum to discuss your childhood dreams of the spires of Oxford or to tell the admissions tutors that your main reason for applying is the excellent reputation of Cambridge. Neither of these, of themselves, is sufficient reason for applying and frankly they've been heard before. It's taken for granted that you know of the reputation of both Oxford and Cambridge and the tutors want facts, not dreams!

Given that the admissions tutors will read both forms, it looks better if you have gone to the trouble of taking advantage of that opportunity.

TAILOR THE INTERVIEW

The key advantage of mentioning areas of special academic interest (and that includes your wider reading), is that it gives you a chance of getting a predictable question at interview which allows you to shine. The key risk you are running is that you won't shine. The interviewer can instantly compare you unfavourably with other candidates who would have been able to answer the question more impressively, given the same background interest and wider reading. Interviews are dealt with in the next chapter, but this section concentrates on what to put in your personal statement. The best advice is to go for it, and just be determined to ensure that you can shine when probed on your interests and your wider reading. If you are in any doubt about this, simply remember that, if you specify no areas of special academic interest, you could very easily be asked to suggest some at interview. Would you rather be prepared or unprepared?

YOUR A LEVELS

Think about your A levels but focus on areas where your knowledge goes beyond the syllabus. Concentrate on the A levels which are most relevant to your proposed degree course. Within an A level subject, concentrate if possible on topics which are relevant to your degree.

The interviewers are much more likely to pick something which they know is relevant to undergraduate study. If you can't think of any such topics, generate some quickly! Pick an area of the syllabus which you understand, which addresses fundamental first principles and questions of theory, which attracts you aesthetically and which, ideally, throws up obvious further questions that the A level syllabus stops short of addressing. After that, there's no substitute for simply going out there and investigating the answers to some of those unresolved questions. That immediately generates wider reading.

The approach is similar if you are applying for a course with components that have no obvious relationship to any of your A level subjects. Examples might include Archaeology and Anthropology, Computing, Human Sciences, Land Economy, Law, Psychology and Philosophy. This time, focus on the degree course content instead of the A level course content, and make use of all the literature that you've obtained from the faculty offices and the bookshops.

DON'T TRY TOO HARD!

You're minimising your risk all the time, so don't blow it by mentioning something in your personal statement that you don't really understand. Chemists have been known to say that they are interested in mechanisms and are looking forward to learning about how quantum theory is going to revolutionise the understanding that they've gained at A level. Quantum theory is pretty difficult and as an A level student you won't get close to the understanding you're going to gain as an undergraduate. So unless you are really knowledgeable on this subject it is best left alone. The trick would be to start with an elementary treatment which you can understand.

KNOW WHAT YOU SAY YOU KNOW

Similarly, if you're applying to read English or, say, Modern Languages, and you wish to mention an author you admire, it is essential that you have read at least two or three of the author's works, that you can talk about genre and that you display critical analysis rather than narrowly focusing on the 'story'. If you decide to mention a field on which you know your interviewer is a world expert, you have to be particularly careful. The interviewer may suspect your tactics and give you just that extra little bit of grilling.

**WRITTEN
TESTS**

MEDICINE AND VETERINARY SCIENCE

All applicants for Medicine, Veterinary Science or
Physiological Sciences at both Cambridge and Oxford (as
well as a number of other university medical departments) must sit the BMAT (Bio-Medical Admissions Test).
The test is sat in November and is designed to gauge a
candidate's aptitude for a Biomedical degree rather then
their flair for practice or advanced factual knowledge. It is
a challenging test in three parts – a 60-minute test of
aptitude and skills, a 30-minute test of scientific knowledge and a 30-minute writing task. Further information is
available at www.bmat.org.uk.

LAW

All applicants for Law at both universities will have to sit
the Law National Admissions Test (LNAT), in November.
The test is in two parts – an 80-minute multiple-choice
paper to assess skills of logic and analysis and a 40-minute
essay. No prior legal knowledge is required. Further
information is available at www.lnat.ac.uk.

HISTORY

Applicants for History at Oxford will take the History
Aptitude Test (HAT). Like the BMAT, it is a challenging
test of aptitude and potential rather than knowledge. It
will last two hours and is based on two extracts. Further
information is available at www.history.ox.ac.uk.

ENGLISH

The English Department at Oxford is currently consider-
ing whether to introduce a written test for English to be
sat pre-interview. Details on the progress of this matter
will be kept at www.english.ox.ac.uk.

MATHEMATICS

All Cambridge colleges except Hughes Hall and Lucy
Cavendish will ask you to sit a Sixth Term Examination
Paper (STEP) if you are applying to read Mathematics. It
is sat in late June through your school and it assesses aptitude for university study in the subject, looking

particularly at qualities like insight and originality. Churchill and Peterhouse may use STEP as part of their conditional offers for Engineering. Churchill may also use it for Computer Science, as may Magdalene.

PHYSICS

Students applying to read Physics or Physics and Philosophy will need to sit a test in Mathematics and Physics at Oxford in November. Further information can be found at www.physics.ox.ac.uk/admissions/newtests.htm.

OTHER SUBJECTS

Some Cambridge colleges may ask you to sit the Thinking Skills Assessment test (TSA) when you come for interview. It assesses critical thinking and problem-solving skills but is not subject specific, although it has been used to assess applicants for Computer Science, Economics, Engineering and Natural Sciences.

You have less, but still some control over the written tests that you may be required to take at the time of interview. The key things to bear in mind are revision of your A level work, getting hold of past papers, practice and exam strategy on the day. This is very much the advice that one would give to students taking any exam, but there are important respects in which the assessment of Oxbridge written tests may differ from that of, say, an A level exam.

In an A level exam, it is crucial that you answer all the questions so that you can accumulate as many points as possible. In an Oxbridge written test, you still have chances if you can show flair, insight and, in the case of Arts subjects, quality of prose style at least somewhere in the test. The assessors are looking for this flair rather than seeing how many marks you can accumulate. If you simply have not covered the material at school, you should say so and move on to a question that you can answer.

A booklet containing specimen tests for Oxford is available from the Oxford Colleges Admission Office. In Cambridge, policy on written tests is more at the college level than the university level, and your best bet is to contact your college to ask for specimen papers. Practise the papers that you are sent and try to have them marked by your school teachers. When going over them, pay more attention to the quality than the quantity of your answers.

Don't expect the same questions to come up in the real thing. But as with written work submitted in advance of the interviews, try to remember the type of questions and what you have written. Even if you only have a few hours before your interview, you would be wise to revisit the questions and analyse how you could have improved upon your answers.

WRITTEN WORK SUBMITTED BEFORE INTERVIEW

The college and subject combinations that require written work to be submitted in advance and/or written tests at interview are dealt with in the Oxford and Cambridge prospectuses. In the case of Oxford, the prospectus details precisely the written work required for each subject. This work has to be sent to the individual college with a cover sheet which is available from your school. Each Cambridge college has its own policy on written work and will write to candidates individually to explain what, if any, written work is required. Here some general advice is given on how to turn the apparent threat into an opportunity.

Written work should usually be submitted by early November, in other words about a fortnight after the deadline for application. The guideline is that the work should have been completed as part of your A level studies and have been marked. Ideally, you want your submissions to represent your most mature work. Coursework is often appropriate. So is work that you have completed in the summer term before making your application, although some departments prefer mock exam scripts written in January or February. You should date any earlier pieces so that the admissions tutors can take this into account. You need to get on the right side of your teachers so that, if necessary, you can submit pieces undertaken specifically with your Oxbridge application in mind.

The colleges are reasonably flexible when it comes to the type of written work submitted, despite the guidelines, and it would be better to submit something, no matter how recently written, than having to rely on poor pieces completed as part of your school homework. Better still, treat every piece of homework that you complete during the lower sixth as a potential Oxbridge submission. It will do your A levels no harm! It is always better to submit work that demonstrates critical insight, complex manipulation of argument or technically demanding skills than to submit work that simply demonstrates that you have regurgitated facts or ploughed through some standard exercises.

Always keep a copy of the work you have submitted; you may be asked further questions about it at interview. If you are called for interview, you would be wise to review the work again, anticipate any criticisms and analyse some of the wider issues it raises.

CHECKLIST

- ☐ Write individual personal statements tailored to each form
- ☐ Emphasise areas of special academic interest for Oxbridge forms
- ☐ Treat every piece of lower-sixth homework as a potential Oxbridge submission
- ☐ Practise past papers for written tests.

INTERVIEWS

Interviews are usually held in early to mid-December. You need to be well presented (although suits are not required), alert and reasonably relaxed in your surroundings. Ideally, you should check in well before your first interview and, if possible, make use of the opportunity to spend the previous evening in college.

There will often be two interviews at your first-choice college, one a specialist interview with subject tutors and the other a more general interview, often with the admissions tutor. Expect the possibility of more than one specialist interview if you are applying for joint honours and sometimes even for single honours. At Oxford, you may well be called for additional interviews at other colleges if you are borderline for your own college, and the final decisions about your application are usually made by Christmas. At Cambridge, 'pool' interviews are held in early January, with final decisions shortly thereafter.

The style and content of the interview varies not only from university to university and college to college, but also from subject to subject and candidate to candidate. There is no such thing as a 'standard' interview. In recent years, the interview process has tended to become less intimidating. Some of this year's candidates were surprised by how well they were looked after during their stays, and by the level of concern that was shown over their welfare. However, don't get lulled into complacency. One candidate tells of how intimidated she felt when, having had a very relaxed introduction to Oxford and a 'chatty' and undemanding first interview, she walked into her subject interview to find seven interviewers seated in a circle, waiting to fire questions at her.

WHY DO THEY INTERVIEW YOU?

The Oxbridge interview is your chance to show that you are more than simply the sum of your qualifications, that you know more than how to revise well and work hard. It allows the interviewers, some of whom will teach you during your three or four years there, to discover your future academic potential. The interviewers are looking to see how much you have absorbed already from your academic work and to see how you use what you know. They are certainly not looking for candidates who already know half the degree course before they have even done their A levels. Rather, they want to know what you can do with what you have already got. You should not therefore be worried about the fact that you know very few technical legal terms or are unsure as to exactly how the latest computer chip works. They are not looking for a walking encyclopedia. On the other hand, your interest in the subject should mean that you have done some investigation into recent studies or issues in your chosen subject and can discuss them to some extent.

THE GENERAL INTERVIEW

At some colleges you may have a non-academic interview. This is often conducted by the admissions tutor, and it is the admissions tutor who makes the final decision on your application – albeit influenced by all the other aspects of your application including, of course, the notes from your specialist interviewers.

This is the interview in which you are most likely to be asked 'Why this university?', 'Why this college?', 'Tell me about *the last book that you read and your extracurricular activities'*, *'What is your reaction to this editorial in today's* Times?' Equally, you may well be asked questions about your proposed degree course, which may strike you as being as exacting as any that you are asked in your specialist interview.

The general interview is an opportunity to show how articulate you are and how quickly you can think on your feet. Draw on all the research that you undertook when choosing your subject, your university and your college. Make sure that you can support and expand upon everything that you have said in your two personal statements and, for at least two weeks beforehand, ensure that you have kept abreast of current affairs, particularly any that touch upon your chosen degree course. Seek practice interviews – preferably from your school or from others with experience of the Oxbridge system but, failing that, from anyone who can duplicate the somewhat adversarial style of a one-to-one verbal examination with you on the receiving end.

Note that Oxford now states that it is more interested in your academic interview and will not spend much time discussing your hobbies, for example, or the latest economic and political news. Before you breathe too big a sigh of relief and throw away your copies of the broadsheets, do remember that a decent knowledge of current affairs can inform your understanding of many subjects, and in interviews for Law, Politics and Economics for example, your interest in the latest governmental problem or legal miscarriage of justice can be of great benefit should you wish to direct the interview or are struggling to answer a question put to you. Remember that reading around your subject, whatever it is, will impress.

THE SPECIALIST INTERVIEW

WHAT DO THEY WANT?

This is the interview about which myths abound in secondary schools all over the world. You will probably remember your specialist interview at Oxbridge for the rest of your life, so make sure you enjoy it! You may find it helpful to psych yourself up into regarding it as a treat — a rare opportunity to command the undivided attention of leading academic experts, and an important foretaste of all the job interviews that you may ever have in the future. If you can relish the experience, you are more likely to display the intellectual curiosity that your interviewers are seeking. What else will they be looking for?

They will be expecting you to have a good understanding of relevant material that you have studied so far at A level. They will be more interested in your grasp of first principles than your memory for facts. They will expect you to have researched at least one or two areas beyond A level, and they will expect you to have done some research on your proposed degree subject and to be able to talk about it analytically and critically. If you can use some technical vocabulary (correctly), you will find that this is a great advantage. They will also be looking for your ability to think on your feet. Finally, they will expect you to be able to remember what you wrote in your written tests and to be able to expand on any written material submitted in advance of the interviews.

PREPARATION

- All these themes are more or less predictable and you can prepare for them. It is remarkable how far preparation and practice can take you, and even more remarkable how little preparation some of your competitors will have done. Start with the following:
- Ask yourself what aspects of the subject attract you.
- Ensure that you are fully up to speed on all the topics you have so far covered in your A levels.
- Make yourself aware of any important recent developments in your chosen subject.
- Think about the reason that your subject is studied.
- Think about your subject's broader application in the real world. How relevant is it to everyday life?
- Go through the prospectus and make sure that you know the course that is on offer. Be prepared to go into some detail as to the aspects of it which have attracted you.

■ On the major topics within your subject, look at the common arguments on both sides. Make sure you understand them all and know which one you agree with. Be prepared to justify your choice.

■ Be fully prepared to discuss the issues which arise from your personal statement.

Don't be surprised if the views that you have expressed are belittled or treated as worthless. Oxbridge is all about education through intellectual perfectionism. Start by defending your views, but listen carefully to the counter-arguments. Ideally, try to suggest the counter-arguments before they are suggested to you. Don't be afraid to criticise the counter-arguments themselves, but dispel from your mind any personal tastes and concentrate instead on issues, definitions, evidence, angle of approach and logic.

HOW TO ANSWER THE DIFFICULT QUESTIONS

First of all, stay calm and remember exactly what it is that the interviewers are trying to achieve. They are not primarily trying to find out what facts you know. They are endeavouring to find out if you have an enquiring mind and if you can apply first principles and the facts that you do know to new problems.

Let us take a question which has been asked at a past Oxbridge interview and go through a possible sequence which might be used in order to answer it.

Should judges be elected?

This is a question which appears to require a definitive answer. Immediately you should be aware that you will need to look at all sides of the argument, whether you agree with them or not, with the final aim of coming down on a particular side if you can.

Are there any words in the question which might need clarification? For example, does the word 'elected' refer to election by the public or by other judges or by politicians even? Start by discussing this. As you speak you are giving yourself both clarification of the issue and more time to think.

Identify the main issues which would arise were judges to be elected. Point out the advantages and disadvantages, all the time putting forward an opinion of your own and, if you have none, put forward those which are generally held if you know them.

It may be impossible for you to come up with an answer you feel happy with. In which case, say so. Explain that you feel the arguments for and against are all persuasive and you do not therefore feel able to answer the question fully. If however you do have an opinion as to the 'correct' answer, give it, ensuring that you reiterate the arguments to back up your choice.

Our approach is not the only method that will enable you to stay calm and give of your best when you get into trouble. It should not distract you from the basics. For example, in interviews for modern languages, expect most of the questions to revolve around your reading, comprehension and translation skills. Remember that, when discussing literature (English or otherwise) the interviewers are more likely to be interested in 'how?' rather than 'what?' For technical questions in mathematics or the physical sciences, you will be better off concentrating on your A level groundwork, identifying fundamental principles, stating what you do know and building from there – relying on the way in which you have presented yourself elsewhere in the interview to buy you some hints. Whichever approach you adopt, though, you will carry it off much more effectively if you have had some practice. Have a go at some of the questions in the next section, ask your teachers for further examples and try to arrange some mock interviews.

WHAT TO DO IF YOU CAN'T ANSWER THE QUESTION

Above all, do not panic!

Firstly, identify what it is about the question that has stopped you in your tracks. Is it that you do not understand the question itself? If so, ask for it to be repeated. If you have no knowledge whatsoever of the topic to which the question refers, ascertain whether there is a related topic about which you do feel confident and say to the interviewer: *'I do not know very much about that particular topic but it seems quite similar to...'* and then go on to discuss that. You can only really do this if there is some relevance in the topic you are trying to lead them to. You can to some extent steer the interview to your advantage and show them where you can shine. Where this is not possible, use the approach described above and this will get you some of the way at least. Whatever you do though, don't try and pretend that you know what you are talking about when you do not have a clue. Far better to be honest and admit your difficulties than to try and pull the wool over your interviewers' eyes. It will invariably fail as these people are leading academics in their chosen field. You will often find that when you are struggling you will be prompted and this will be all that you need to get back on track.

ANY QUESTIONS?

Sometimes, you will be asked at the end of your interview if there are any questions that you would like to put. 'No, thank you' is a perfectly acceptable, no-risk reply. Alternatively, if you wish to ask specific questions about your course or college, which you haven't found answers to despite undertaking all the research that has been suggested, the chances are that the question is worth asking. Don't ask it, though, if you aren't really interested in the answer and couldn't develop the conversation further. One of the braver things that you can do is to ask a question arising from an earlier part of the technical discussion. That can be a good strategy if you felt that you underperformed on a technical question and could have done better. But it can be a risky strategy if the interviewer thinks that you're forcing yourself.

PHYSICAL FACTORS

Remember to look at the interviewers when you are answering their questions. Practise on friends who are making Oxbridge applications themselves. Swap roles with each other and get used to answering questions in connected sentences, each of which paves the way for the one that follows. Try to avoid slang such as *'like'*, *'yeah'* and *'you know'*. Practise smiling and eye contact, both of which not only give the impression of engaging with your interviewer but also genuinely assist the process of concentrating on the precise question that you have been asked.

PSYCHOLOGICAL FACTORS

Being in the right frame of mind is important. Keep reminding yourself that, if you have revised all the relevant A level material, have wider reading that you can talk about and have practised a little, you are likely to perform to the best of your ability. Remember to enjoy the interview experience as much as possible without appearing casual, and to defend your views without appearing arrogant or blinkered. If you are incredibly nervous, that won't be held against you. (Some of the world's greatest academics are extremely nervous people!) If a question appears to be trivial, bear in mind that it probably isn't. If a question appears to be impossible, then in the worst case maintain your intellectual curiosity.

■ Consider the obvious questions which could be asked, such as why you want to study the particular subject you have applied for and why you want to study at Oxford or Cambridge.

■ Read through the written work that you submitted and think about the questions which may arise from it. Look particularly at how you might expand upon what you wrote.

■ Ensure that you have read beyond any texts set for A level and that you are up to date with any very recent developments in your subject. If you are questioned on any of these, you will need to be able to discuss them in a thoughtful and critical manner.

■ Practise interviews with friends if you can, but preferably they should be with someone you do not know well, for example a tutor at school who does not teach you.

SAMPLE QUESTIONS

The following are real questions that have been asked of Oxbridge applicants over the past few years. The college and university names have been omitted and the specialist interview questions have been subdivided by subject. For brevity, the topic is sometimes given rather than the whole series of actual questions which were asked. Several of the questions were linked to material on the prior written tests. Remember that it's pointless mugging up responses to these specialist questions. Their function is to enable you to plan the best method of practising the task that lies ahead of you.

GENERAL INTERVIEW QUESTIONS

- Why this college?
- What are you intending to do in your gap year?
- Excluding your A level reading, what were the last three books you read?
- What defines a novel as Gothic?
- I notice that you have a grade B in Biology GCSE. Should we be worried about that?
- Give a critical appraisal of the main broadsheet newspaper that you read.
- What do you regard as your strengths and weaknesses?
- What extracurricular activities would you pursue at this college?
- Do you realise that you have applied for the most popular college at this university?
- Why did you make an open application?
- What do you think of Labour's discrimination in favour of female parliamentarians?
- How would you improve the comprehensive system of education?
- Give us three reasons why we should offer you a place.
- What will you do if we don't?
- What are the synergies, if any, between your three A level subjects?
- So, is it the case that you only want to come to this university but don't care what you do?
- Why did you choose your A level subjects?
- Name one weakness you have and explain how you would rectify it.
- How will this degree help in your chosen career?

■ Do you believe that you have an adventurous side?

■ Do you find it daunting not knowing what you will be doing in four or five years' time?

■ How would your friends describe you?

■ Why are you having to retake your A level(s)? What happened last year?

SPECIALIST INTERVIEW QUESTIONS

ANTHROPOLOGY/ARCHAEOLOGY

■ How do you feel about having to study both Anthropology and Archaeology during your first year before choosing one?

■ Name the six major world religions.

■ Does Stonehenge mean anything to you?

■ What are the problems regarding objectivity in anthropological studies?

■ Why do civilisations erect monuments?

■ Why should we approach all subjects from an holistic, anthropological perspective?

ART HISTORY

■ What do we look for when we study Art? What are we trying to reveal?

■ Comment on this painting on the wall.

■ Compare and contrast these three images.

■ What exhibitions have you been to recently?

■ Why did you choose your A level subjects?

■ How can you classify whether a piece of art is successful or not?

■ Do we theorise too much about art?

■ Why History of Art?

■ How does History of Art help you to break down barriers and communicate with people?

■ Does knowing languages help you communicate with the inhabitants of the country?

■ Compare the study of the Renaissance with that of the French Revolution.

■ Apart from your studies, how else might you pursue your interest in Art History while at the university?

BIOCHEMISTRY

- *Questions on catalysts, enzymes and the chemistry of the formation of proteins.*
- *Questions on oxidation, equilibria and interatomic forces.*
- *Questions on X-ray crystallography.*
- Why do you wish to read Biochemistry rather than Chemistry?
- *Current issues in Biochemistry.*

BIOLOGICAL SCIENCES

- How does the immune system recognise invading pathogens as foreign cells?
- How does a cell stop itself from exploding due to osmosis?
- Why is carbon of such importance in living systems?
- How would you transfer a gene to a plant?
- Explain the mechanism of capillary action.
- What are the advantages of the human genome project?
- How would you locate a gene in a nucleus of a cell for a given characteristic?
- What is the major problem with heart transplants in the receiver?
- How does the transplant receiver respond to foreign heart cells?
- How does the body recognise and distinguish its own cells from the foreign cells after a transplant?

CHEMISTRY

- *Questions on organic mechanisms.*
- *Questions on structure, bonding and energetics.*
- *Questions on acids and bases.*
- *Questions on isomerisation.*
- *Questions on practical chemical analysis.*
See also Biochemistry questions.

CLASSICS

- *Questions on classical civilisation and literature.*
- Why do you think Ancient History is important?

■ How civilised was the Roman world?

■ Apart from your A level texts, what have you read in the original or in translation?

EARTH SCIENCES AND GEOLOGY

■ Where would you place this rock sample in geological time?

■ How would you determine its age?

■ Can you integrate this decay curve, and why would the result be useful?

■ *Questions on Chemistry.*

■ When do you think oil will run out?

ECONOMICS

■ Explain how the Phillips curve arises.

■ Would it be feasible to have an economy which was entirely based on the service sector?

■ A man pays for his holiday at a hotel on a tropical island by cheque. He has a top credit rating and rather than cashing it, the hotelier pays a supplier using the same cheque. That supplier does the same thing with one of his suppliers and so on ad infinitum. Who pays for the man's holiday?

■ Discuss the interaction between fiscal and monetary policy.

■ I notice that you study Mathematics. Can you see how you might derive the profit maximisation formula from first principles?

■ Discuss competition in the TV industry.

■ How effective is current monetary policy?

■ What are your particular interests as regards economics?

■ Do you think we should worry about a balance of payments deficit?

■ If you were the Chancellor of the Exchequer, how would you maximise tax revenue?

■ If you had a fairy godmother who gave you unlimited sums of money, what sort of company would you start and what types of employee would you hire?

■ What are the advantages and disadvantages of joining the Euro?

- What are the qualities of a good economist?
- Why are you studying Economics A level?
- What would happen to employment and wage rates if the pound depreciated?

ENGINEERING

- *Questions on Mathematics and Physics, particularly calculus and mechanics.*
- *Questions on mathematical derivations, eg of laws of motion.*
- This mechanical system sitting on my desk – how does it work?
- How do aeroplanes fly?
- What is impedance matching and how can it be achieved?
- How do bicycle spokes work?
- How would you divide a tetrahedron into two identical parts?
- What is the total resistance of the tetrahedron if there are resistors of one ohm on each edge?
- Questions on Hooke's law.

ENGLISH

- What is the most important work of literature of the 20th century?
- Who is your favourite author?
- Do you do any creative writing? Do you keep a diary? Do you write letters?
- Discussion of reading beyond your A level texts.
- Provide a review of the last Shakespeare play you saw at the theatre.
- Examine the hypothesis that Shakespeare was unusually atheistic for his time.
- *Questions on deconstruction of a poem.*
- *Questions on the use of language.*
- Are Iago and Othello good listeners?
- Discuss the last novel you read.

GEOGRAPHY

- Is Geography just a combination of other disciplines?
- Why should it be studied in its own right?

- Would anything remain of Geography if we took the notion of place off the syllabus?
- How important is the history of towns when studying settlement patterns?
- Why is climate so unpredictable?

See also questions on Land Economy.

HISTORY

- *Questions on historical themes and movements.*
- How can one define revolution?
- Why did imperialism happen?
- What were the differences between German and Italian unification?
- Who was the greater democrat – Gladstone or Disraeli?
- Was the fall of the Weimar Republic inevitable?
- 'History is the study of the present with the benefit of hindsight.' Discuss.
- Would history be worth studying if it didn't repeat itself?
- What is the difference between Modern History and Modern Politics?
- What is the position of the individual in history?
- Would you abolish the monarchy for ideological or practical reasons?
- Should we abolish the House of Lords?
- Should we elect the second chamber?
- Why do historians differ in their views on Hitler?
- What skills should a historian have?
- In what periods has the Holy Grail been popular, with whom and why?
- Why do you think the Holy Grail gains more attention during certain periods?
- Why is it important to visit historical sites relevant to the period you are studying?

HUMAN SCIENCES

- Discuss BSE and its implications, and the role of prions in CJD.
- What causes altitude sickness and how do humans adapt physiologically to high altitudes?

- Discuss exploitation of indigenous populations by Westerners.
- Why is statistics a useful subject for human scientists?
- Why are humans so difficult to experiment with?
- Design an experiment to determine whether genetics or upbringing is more important.
- What are the scientific implications of globalisation on the world?

LAND ECONOMY

- Will the UK lose its sovereignty if it joins EMU?
- Will EMU encourage regionalism?
- Will the information technology revolution gradually result in the death of inner cities?
- What has been the effect of the Channel tunnel on surrounding land use?

LAW

- *Questions on written cases, judgments and arguments.*
- *Questions on the points of law arising from scenarios — often relating to criminal law or duty of care.*
- A cyclist rides the wrong way down a one-way street and a chimney falls on him. What legal proceedings should he take?
- What if he is riding down a private drive signed 'no trespassing'?
- X intends to poison his wife but accidentally gives the lethal draught to her identical twin. Murder?
- *Questions on legal issues, particularly current ones.*
- Should stalking be a criminal offence?
- Should judges have a legislative role?
- Do you think that anyone should be able to serve on a jury?
- Should judges be elected?
- Do judges have political bias?
- To what extent do you think the press should be able to release information concerning allegations against someone?
- Is there anything you want to discuss or that you're really interested in?
- Euthanasia — who has the right to decide?

■ How does the definition of intent distinguish murder from manslaughter?

■ Can you give a definition of murder and manslaughter?

■ Should foresight of consequences be considered as intending such consequences?

MATERIAL SCIENCES

■ *Questions on Physics, particularly solid materials.*

■ *Questions on Mathematics, particularly forces.*

■ *Investigations of sample materials, particularly structure and fractures.*

MATHEMATICS AND COMPUTATION

■ *Questions (which may become progressively harder) on almost any area of A level maths and further maths.*

■ *Pure maths questions on integration.*

■ *Applied maths questions on forces.*

■ *Statistics questions on probability.*

■ *Computation questions on iterations, series and computer arithmetic.*

MEDICINE

■ What did your work experience teach you about life as a doctor?

■ What did you learn about asthma in your work experience on asthma research?

■ How have doctors' lives changed in the last 30 years?

■ Explain the logic behind the most recent of the NHS reforms.

■ Discuss the mechanisms underlying diabetes.

■ Why is it that cancer cells are more susceptible to destruction by radiation than normal cells?

■ How would you determine whether leukemia patients have contracted the disease because of a nearby nuclear power station?

■ What does isometric exercise mean in the context of muscle function?

■ Discuss the mechanisms underlying sensory adaptation.

■ What is an ECG?

■ Why might a GP not prescribe antibiotics to a toddler?

■ Why are people anxious before surgery? Is it justifiable?

■ How do you deal with stress?

■ *Questions on gene therapy.*

■ *Questions on the ethics of foetal transplantation.*

■ *Questions on Biochemistry and Human Biology.*

MODERN LANGUAGES

■ Tests and questions on comprehension and translation.

■ Reading tests.

■ *Questions which focus on the use of language in original texts.*

■ *Questions on cultural and historical context and genre in European literature.*

■ How important is analysis of narrative in the study of literature?

■ How important is biography in the study of literature?

NATURAL SCIENCES

■ What is an elastic collision?

■ What happens when two particles collide – one moving and one stationary?

■ What is friction?

■ *Questions on carboxylic acids.*

ORIENTAL STUDIES

■ What do you know about the Chinese language and its structure?

■ What are the differences between English and any Oriental language with which you are familiar?

■ Compare and contrast any ambiguities in the following sentences:

   ☐ Only suitable magazines are sold here.

   ☐ Many species inhabit a small space.

   ☐ He is looking for the man who crashed his car.

■ Comment on the following sentences:

   ☐ He did wrong.

   ☐ He was wrong.

   ☐ He was about to do wrong.

PHILOSOPHY

- What is Philosophy?
- Give examples of philosophical questions.
- Would you agree that if p is true and s believes p, then s knows p?
- Is the above a question about knowing or a question about the meaning of the word *know*?
- Discuss:
  - ☐ I could be dreaming that I am in this interview.
  - ☐ I do not know whether I am dreaming or not.
  - ☐ Therefore I do not know whether I am in this interview or not.
- Can a machine have free will?
- When I see red, could I be seeing what you see when you see green?
- Is it a matter of fact or logic that time travels in one direction only?
- Is our faith in scientific method itself based on scientific method? If so, does it matter?
- I can change my hairstyle and still be me. I can change my political opinions and still be me. I can have a sex change and still be me. What is it then that makes me be me?
- Can it ever be morally excusable to kill someone?

PHYSICS

- *Questions on Applied Mathematics.*
- *Questions on any aspect of the Physics syllabus.*
- *Questions on mathematical derivations.*
- How does glass transmit light?
- How does depressing a piano key make a sound?
- How does the voltage on a capacitor vary if the dielectric gas is ionised?

POLITICS

- Define government. Why do we need governments?
- Differentiate between power and authority.
- Distinguish between a society, a state and an economy.
- Will Old Labour ever be revived? If so, under what circumstances?

- Why do you think that Communism was unsuccessful in the Russian countryside?
- What would you say to someone who claims that women already have equal opportunities?
- What would you do tomorrow if you were the president of the former Soviet Union?
- How does a democracy work?
- What constitute the ideologies of the extreme right?
- Does the extreme right pose a threat to other less extreme parties?

POLITICS, PHILOSOPHY AND ECONOMICS
- Define power, authority and influence.
- How important is national identity? What is the Scottish national identity?
- Should medics pay more for their degrees?
- What is the difference in the mentality of Americans in 1760 and 1770?

PSYCHOLOGY
- *Questions on Neurophysiology.*
- *Questions on Statistics.*
- *Questions on the experimental elucidation of the mechanisms underlying behaviour.*
- Give some examples of why an understanding of Chemistry might be important in Psychology.
- A new treatment is tested on a group of depressives, who are markedly better in six weeks. Does this show that the treatment was effective?
- There are records of violent crimes that exactly mimic scenes of violence on TV. Does this indicate that TV causes real violence?
- How would you establish the quietest sound that you can hear as opposed to the quietest sound that you think you can hear?
- Why might one be able to remember items at the beginning and end of an aurally presented list better than items in the middle?
- Could a computer ever feel emotion?
- Is it ethically justifiable to kill animals for the purpose of research?
- What is emotional intelligence?

SOCIAL AND POLITICAL SCIENCES

- What is the value of the study of Social Anthropology?
- Do people need tabloids?
- How would you define terrorism?
- Do you believe in selective education? Are we participating in selective education here?
- Is it possible to pose a sociological problem without sociological bias?
- Does prison work?
- Are MPs only in it for the power?
- What aspects of the subject are you particularly looking forward to studying?

See also questions on Politics.

THEOLOGY

- Does moral rectitude reside in the agent, the act or its consequences?
- What, if anything, is wrong with voluntary euthanasia?
- What is the best reason that you can think of for believing in the existence of God?
- Do you think that this course could conceivably be persuasive on the issue?
- What relevance does Theology have for Art History?
- What relevance does Archaeology have for Theology?
- Comment on the portrayal of Jesus in John versus the other gospels.

VETERINARY MEDICINE

- Should the veterinary profession show positive discrimination in favour of men?
- Has your work experience influenced your future career aspirations?
- Discuss any aspect of animal physiology which has struck you as contrasting with what you know of human physiology.
- Would our knowledge of BSE have been of value in controlling foot-and-mouth disease?
- Discuss the biochemistry of DNA.
- What animal did this skull belong to?

See also questions on Biological Sciences and Chemistry.

7

SOME STUDENT EXPERIENCES

Even if you have read this book several times from cover to cover, done all the research that has been recommended and sorted out some mock interviews, you will still lack the knowledge of hindsight. That omission cannot be repaired, but applicants may find it useful to hear about some firsthand experiences. The following case histories, again arising from specialist interviews that have taken place during the past few years, will hopefully enable you to tie together some of the recurring themes in this book. With luck, though, you will not have been prevented from going into your interview with the sense of curiosity and trepidation appropriate in someone embarking upon a life where there will always be more to learn than you already know.

NISHA

'I was very concerned about my interview. I had applied post A level and felt that I had a great deal to prove, especially as one of my A levels was particularly disappointing and I knew I would have to do some explaining to justify myself. I wasn't, however, as nervous as I think I would have been had I applied before I had done my A levels. At least I had gained some experience in the big wide world and felt fairly confident about my current intelligence, if not about my performance in the A levels the previous summer – although I had also achieved an S grade in the English STEP!

'True to form, my first interview was incredibly tense, with the interviewer doing very little to encourage me either way. As I answered her questions I was never able to really assess from her reaction whether or not I was on the right track. She was determined to keep away from discussing any of the texts which I had studied for the exams, but as an English student I ought to have guessed this would happen. She asked some incredibly searching questions and some incredibly open questions which actually gave me an opportunity to talk freely and without constraint.

'The second interviewer was more affable and open and the interview felt more like a two-way discussion as opposed to the previous "grilling"! We discussed the written paper which I had been given to do before the interview. I was asked why I had chosen to do the questions I had attempted. I was also given a practical criticism to do there and then with no time for preparation. At no point did I feel that this interviewer was trying to catch me out. He was incredibly open with me although his questions were as searching in more technical terms as the previous one. At times though, he spoke over me which I found a little rude – but I was not frightened to ask him to let me finish. I was not prepared to be pushed around! Overall this was a friendly and encouraging interview.

'I then had the general admissions interview, where I had to justify my poor grade in the History A level. This was a very cold interview – I felt very unnerved by the interviewer's attitude. She asked me why I had chosen the college and what I felt about the fact that it was single sex.

'Overall the whole experience left me with a mixture of feelings from resentment at being talked over to elation at having been able to discuss in-depth the subject I loved with people who clearly loved it as much as I did and knew so much more than I did. I was offered a place.'

COMMENTARY

Nisha was fortunate to be called for interview with a poor A level grade in her portfolio and the thought of having to explain it quite understandably made her very nervous. In this situation, as long as there really are good reasons rather than pure laziness on your part, this is something you should be happy to answer as long as you do so honestly. There is no shame in admitting that you were not able to work at the necessary level for the course at that particular time in your life or that you now feel that you chose the wrong course. Just be honest.

Nisha appeared quite surprised at being asked about so many texts which were not on the syllabus, but as an English applicant she should have been absolutely prepared to do this. All literature-based courses require undergraduates with a natural interest in their subject and the ability to focus on issues and topics without prompting.

Nisha was undoubtedly a strong candidate as she does not appear to have been put out at all by the prospect of undertaking a practical criticism without having been given the time to prepare for it. Nor was she at all disconcerted by the interviewer talking over her. Although this hopefully does not happen on a regular basis, you perhaps should bear in mind that it may well happen and you should therefore be prepared for it. This candidate obviously had enough confidence in her own abilities to ensure that she was allowed to get across the points which she wanted, regardless of the intentions of the

interviewer! Her confidence obviously impressed as she
was offered a place.

SONIA

'As I waited to be called, I chatted to the other girls
who were waiting with me. Everyone was very
nervous but also friendly and surprisingly supportive. The first thing we were asked to do was a
written test on grammar. It was incredibly hard:
about the same level as the STEP which I took later
that year. It lasted about an hour and there was no
time to look up and see how anyone else was doing.

'After that I saw the Admissions Tutor. She was terribly calm and simply asked me gentle questions
about why I wanted to come to that college and
what I hoped to gain from it. We talked in a general
way about some recent items in the news, and that
was it. She seemed to be there to keep us calm.

'The second interview was about one hour after the
first and involved two members of the Modern and
Medieval Languages department. They asked me
about my A level subjects and in particular my
French. I had to explain why I enjoyed it yet did
not want to continue studying it. I also had to read
aloud a piece of French prose and explain how I
would adapt it for television. I was completely
thrown by that question but I stayed calm and
spoke as the ideas came into my head. I am sure
that what I said was total nonsense but at the time I
believed in the ideas and put that confidence
across. Both of the interviewers were very quiet
and gave me no idea of how they viewed what I
said. They smiled a lot but did not really guide me
through, so I could very well have dug myself into a
huge hole.

'For the third interview I was asked to take some
time to read over an article in Spanish which discussed the hypocrisy of war. After a short time I
was called in to meet the two interviewers who

greeted me in Spanish and asked me to comment on the article. As I had never thought about the hypocrisy of war in English let alone Spanish, I really had to think on my feet. They were very helpful though and commented favourably as we went along. They also asked me why I wanted to take up a new language. This interview seemed more like a discussion than the previous one.'

Note that STEP exams are now only requested by Cambridge for Mathematics applicants.

COMMENTARY

This case history should put those who have good academic credentials at ease. The impression reading Sonia's story is that the interviews were not particularly spectacular, nor did she perform spectacularly well in them. For this particular application to read Modern and Medieval Languages at Cambridge (Sonia subsequently took Law as Part II of Tripos), it was the candidate's basic ability, as evidenced by her written tests and her linguistic versatility (and presumably also her GCSE grades and reference) that proved the dominant factors.

The applicant recounts her experiences quite modestly, criticising herself where criticism was probably not really due. This modesty is likely to have come through in a positive way at interview. Notice that she says that the written test in Spanish was incredibly hard, but she does not say that she couldn't do it. She says that she had never really thought about the hypocrisy of war in English (really?) let alone Spanish, but she does not say that she underperformed on this part of the interview. She probably did rather well on it.

It seems likely that Sonia was a strong linguist for whom the interview would not have been critical unless she had genuinely underperformed in it. The admissions tutors retained the protection of being able to demand high grades in the STEPs later that year, and Sonia sailed through.

ANDY

'I remember that I seemed to have to send in lots of work beforehand – much more than some of my friends. The Maths was from my mock exam which I thought was pointless as the papers were, I'm sure, much easier than the standard they were expecting and I had had virtually full marks on some of them. I suppose it showed them how I wrote out my mathematical answers and how many lines I could miss out. The written work was presumably for the Philosophy but as I was doing Science A levels I didn't know what to send. My teachers advised me to send some Physics from my option paper, which was reasonably wordy, and I also did a Philosophy essay at the last minute on Bertrand Russell's *Problems of Philosophy* which wasn't marked.

'At the interviews I did some more Maths tests, which were again of A level standard, and a Philosophy test which I can't remember much about as I was not asked about it at interview. I remember that it involved analysing sentences and that you had to think quite laterally to avoid running out of ideas.

'I wanted my Philosophy interview to be first because I thought it would be easier. In fact it was the other way round and the Philosophy interview was harder. In the first interview, I had to do a lot of integrations and some questions on logs. They asked me if I had any trouble not being allowed a calculator, which I didn't as that is how I had been taught. That seemed to go down very well with them. The integrals were all reciprocals of polynomials. I made a mess of one of them which I thought was a substitution and needed a hint to realise that it was much easier. Then there was a harder one which involved a cubic in the denominator, which wasn't on the A level syllabus. Luckily I had looked at some of them before for interest, and I think this was the best part of the interview. They also asked me to sketch some of the functions, which I think I did well. Apart from the question about calculators, they didn't ask me about the written Maths test. I got the impression that they had marked it though.

'The Philosophy interview was much worse. They said they liked my essay but they picked up on an aspect of induction which I had completely missed, and all the way through I didn't really understand what they were getting at. Then they asked me some questions on definite descriptions like 'the man who stole my wallet'. I only know that they are definite descriptions now, having studied philosophical logic, but I think that I managed to give the impression of following what they were saying, although in fact I wasn't. I managed to remember to try to interrupt them from time to time with other examples which I'd thought of, which seemed to work quite well.

'I enjoyed the whole interview experience and was ecstatic when they offered me a place. It was the best moment of my life and just before Christmas. For my subject (Maths and Philosophy), I would really recommend revising all the Maths syllabus first and doing as much Philosophy reading as possible beforehand.'

COMMENTARY

Andy's dilemma over what written work to submit is not uncommon. The fact that Oxford University was prepared to accept the unmarked work on *Problems of Philosophy* shows the flexibility that admissions tutors are willing to grant in the interests of finding the best students. The fact that the applicant had done this wider reading, and was sufficiently interested in his course to write an essay on it, would have counted in his favour.

This applicant comes across as rather more arrogant than the previous one. He would not have been wise to show such flippancy about the difficulty of the Maths tests at interview. That said, the evidence is that he was probably quite a strong mathematician who also had the advantage of being well taught. He had clearly been taught, for example, not to rely on the crutches of calculators and formulae booklets. The interviewers found that impressive despite almost certainly spotting that his lack of reliance on these crutches was probably an accident of good teaching.

Andy was fortunate to get away with making a mistake on what appears to have been the integral of the reciprocal of a quadratic function. He should have been able to do that question standing on his head, given that he had clearly covered integration at school and was an Oxbridge applicant for a tough honours school. His redemption through the harder integral that came next provides a good example of how important it is to stay focused in the face of embarrassment.

He didn't perform as well in the Philosophy interview. Andy should have taken the written test more seriously – certainly sufficiently seriously to have been able to remember the questions. He was lucky that they didn't ask him again about the sentences that he had to analyse. These questions were almost certainly much less trivial than he realised given that the ability to think laterally about language is a crucial skill in Philosophy.

It is not clear whether or not this applicant had had any mock interviews, but it seems likely. When he had to 'bluff' his way through the argument about induction and, later, definite descriptions, he was able to do so – at least to the satisfaction of the interviewers who subsequently offered him a place. They would almost certainly have seen through the bluffing, but it wasn't critical. The applicant's interview technique was adequate, no doubt helped by practising such situations beforehand.

In summary, this applicant's interviews were not quite such a formality as Sonia's. Andy was clearly an able candidate but he needed to perform in the interview as well, and did just enough.

ROBERT

'I applied for Experimental Psychology at Oxford. I had to send in written work, and chose Biology and English since I thought that I was unusual in doing those two A levels together. With hindsight, now that I am doing the course, I would have sent in some Statistics. Statistics is an important part of the Psychology course in the first year and lots of my friends who didn't take Maths A level have trouble with it. I also had to do a written test, which was a long article on nerves – not a subject which I had studied in Biology.

'At the interview, I was asked about the article and how easy I had found it to understand. Although I said that I had found it hard going and that I had run out of time when doing the test, the interviewer nevertheless launched into a whole string of questions about action potentials and waves of depolarisation. At each stage I had the impression of getting something right and something wrong. The interviewer was very good at explaining each point that I had not quite grasped so that I had a basis for answering the next question. She then asked me what I thought this had to do with Psychology, which I was beginning to wonder myself! It was a good baptism by fire for the scientific content of the course. I think that I answered the question quite well. I realised that Neurophysiology was a core part of the course and that Perception, for example, could be explained in either physiological or psychological terms.

'She then started asking me to relate all this to some visual illusions that she showed me. At first I thought that she was expecting me to talk about action potentials again, but in fact she was getting at physiological and psychological explanations of illusions. I had done some reading on Gregory's explanations and did quite well on the psychological side. But I struggled to see what might have been happening in the eye to explain the illusions. She showed me some fascinating computer models of what was going on in the eye, and how the stimulus fed through the computer program to produce the image of the illusion. I was so genuinely interested in this that I think it had a good effect on her. I spotted the point that the success of the computer model, which was operating at the sensory level, went against cognitive models that explained the illusions in terms of our expectations.

'She then asked me if I had done any other reading around Psychology and I mentioned memory. We had a good discussion, which I had essentially prepared, and I was able to say most of what I had rehearsed. Her questions on this section were not as testing as before, but she did make some thought-provoking comments on which models of memory were actually realistic in terms of what went on in the brain, which brought the topic back to physiology again. The interview went on much longer than I had expected and I got the impression that she was enjoying teaching me, which I remember my tutors at college telling me was important. I think that played a large part in her offering me a place.'

COMMENTARY

This is an example where the interview was probably critical to the offer of a place. At the very least, the specialist interview will have added significantly to any positive impressions gleaned from the rest of the application.

Robert actually had a set of A levels (Mathematics with Statistics, Biology and English) which provided a more or less ideal fit with Psychology at Oxford. He doesn't seem to have realised this himself. At the time he thought that the selling point was that his A level combination was slightly unusual. Good A level fit does applicants no harm at all (see Chapter 2). It is also worth noting parenthetically how scientific the Psychology course at Oxford is. Robert's written tests and specialist interview were dominated by issues of Biology and scientific method. He also chose a college, either through good luck or good management, where the fellow's own research interests were clearly in this direction, illustrating the importance of knowing about your interviewer's specialism just in case it proves important.

Another strong feature of this interview was Robert's demonstration that he had seen through to some of the fundamental issues raised by his prior reading around the subject. Many prospective Psychology students have read Gregory, but Robert's grasp of the different levels of explanation of visual illusions shows particularly mature thinking, and the interview was the only opportunity that he had to demonstrate it. He grasped his opportunity well.

The final feature of this interview which bears mention is the rapport which Robert was able to form with the interviewer. As we have said elsewhere in this guide, it's a major plus if you can come across as someone whom the tutor will enjoy teaching. That the interview lasted longer than expected was a good sign, as was the fact that the interviewer took the trouble to show the applicant a computer demonstration which was probably not part of her prior fixed agenda. The applicant clearly displayed the level of intellectual curiosity that interviewers find so attractive.

MELISSA

'I had two interviews which seemed to me more like discussions than any sort of interrogation, as I had been led to believe they would be by my school. I had undertaken a mock interview in order to prepare and I was pleased that I had because its style had prepared me for the worst! When I arrived, the undergraduates at the college were incrediby helpful, as they were able to give me an insight into what my interviewers were like and they told me what little they could remember of their own interviews too.

'The first interview lasted around 30 minutes and took place in an office just big enough for the two of us. The interviewer started by telling me about himself and some recent research he had been doing – I was so shocked by this as I had expected everything to be about me! It was very effective, though, as it calmed me down as it was so like an ordinary conversation. He then proceeded to ask me why I had chosen this subject over others that might have seemed more obvious for someone with my A levels. We then moved on to some technical questions, one of which involved me commenting on a graph portraying the age of death in certain countries. As I had not looked at this beforehand I had to think on my feet. He had looked at the work I had sent in, and asked me to look at how one of the essays related to the subject I was applying for. He let me talk on about this for what seemed like ages and asked me lots about it. He seemed interested but maybe he was just a good actor!

'In the second interview, I felt far more challenged but not in a confrontational way. When I was asked a question and gave an answer the interviewer would ask me yet another question on my answer in order to take me deeper into the subject matter. A common question she asked was "Why?" It was a very stimulating interview and she seemed genuinely interested in what I had to say. Although I think I tackled much of it well on my own I do think that my better analysis was prompted by her questions and the general discussion.

'Both the interviewers were very hospitable and seemed to be keen to find my strengths rather than my weaknesses. On the whole, I suppose I actually enjoyed the experience!'

COMMENTARY

Melissa was surprised at how relaxed her interviews for Human Sciences were and although the view should not be taken that every interview is a breeze, her experience is an excellent example to dispel the myths which surround the interview process of the two universities. She was disconcerted at the interviewer talking about his own work and although cynics may see this as a method of wrong footing the candidate, it is just as likely that he genuinely wanted to keep the candidate relaxed.

Melissa says that she was allowed to talk about her essay for a very long time. It is worth noting that had she not prepared thoroughly she would not have been able to talk on it for long! It is imperative that you are completely familiar with any work which is sent in to the admissions tutor. Look at any angles which were not covered in the title and try to foresee questions which could commonly arise from it. The idea that your best answers come out when you are challenged by the interviewer goes to the heart of the interview process.

Melissa seemed concerned that she was unable to give her best without prompting, but it is exactly this potential that the tutors are looking for. They seek potential so if you show it, under pressure or otherwise, then you are giving them what they want. They obviously saw Melissa's potential as she was offered a place.

GRACE

'When I arrived at Oxford for the interview I was terribly nervous. I was taken through to a small study where two female professors were sitting. As soon as I walked in, I could sense that the atmosphere was much more relaxed than I had imagined it would be.

'The initial questions they asked me were drawn from points I had made in my personal statement, many of them about the Holy Grail. This immediately made me feel more relaxed as I was confident about being able to support what I had written in my personal statement.

'It was clear to me that they were not trying to trick me by asking questions about historical periods I hadn't covered. They were far more interested in the periods I had covered and were trying to engage me in debate by contradicting a number of the arguments I put forward in response to their questions.

'After around 20 minutes, the questions became focused on an essay I had submitted prior to the interview. The questions were designed to make me look at alternative arguments to those I had used in my essay, and they made me question whether my arguments were right. However, when one of the interviewers asked me a question that seemed to have numerous correct answers, I realised that they were more interested in my ability to analyse different points of view.

'I enjoyed my interview but I was not offered a place.'

COMMENTARY

Grace's interview appears to have gone well. She was nervous of course, but she knew she was capable of answering the interviewers' questions to a high standard. However, the questions focused primarily on one point from her personal statement – her interest in the Holy Grail – and for Grace this narrow scope is why her interview went awry. She felt that she was not given the opportunity to show and discuss her wider historical knowledge.

When an interview seems to be rather one tracked, it is acceptable for an interviewee to attempt to steer the conversation towards a related but different topic by saying, for example, 'Yes, I have looked into that but I have found that my interest lies more in...'

Despite a good interview, an excellent personal statement and a strong reference, Grace was rejected. Unfortunately good candidates do have to be rejected because there are simply not enough places and it would appear that this was the case for Grace.

MONICA

Monica applied to read Modern Languages at Oxford. She had two interviews: one for Spanish, and one for French. Had she applied for joint schools, eg French and Philosophy, she would have had a third 'general' interview. Monica was also given a grammar test, lasting half an hour, for each language. These were fairly straightforward and did not demand knowledge superior to that required for A level.

Her Spanish interview was conducted in three parts. First they talked for a few minutes in Spanish. The questions were fairly standard, 'Why do you want to study languages?' and 'Why Oxford?' Monica found the professor's accent difficult to understand at first but she just asked him to repeat what he'd said. He then asked her, in English, to comment on any texts she had read. Monica handled this badly, choosing a novel that she did not really enjoy and then mumbling something about its unique structure. Finally they moved on to a poem that Monica had been given prior to the interview. The professor asked her what she thought of it but made very few comments on her responses, which Monica found disconcerting.

For the French interview Monica had two interviewers who were much more vivacious. The interview was more challenging and better organised. Again, it was done in three parts. At the start one of the professors mentioned her essay on Maupassant and said that she had enjoyed it. She was about to ask her questions on it but as Monica was more familiar with Camus's *L'Etranger* she asked to discuss this novel instead. They then turned to a 19th-century French poem that had been handed out a few hours before the interview. Monica had panicked when she first saw the poem, because the language was rich in metaphor. She found that her better comments and analysis resulted from discussion, and were prompted by searching questions. The interviewers' questions took her deeper into the intricacies of the poem's structure, choice of metaphor and techniques. The question 'Why?' was a popular one. This was a very stimulating part of the interview as she felt the interviewers Monica's interviews were taking a keen interest in what she said. She was then asked to speak in French. The basis for discussion was an article from *Le Monde*. This was also pre-released material so she could prepare ideas and French phrases beforehand.

COMMENTARY

Monica found communication in her first interview difficult, mostly due to a lack of eye contact and feedback from the professor. At the end of the interview she felt dissatisfied. She didn't feel that she had made many intelligent comments or that she had been encouraged to do so. She was impressed with the freedom to choose any Spanish text for discussion, although disappointed that she didn't make the most of it. She spent the few hours before her next interview wondering how the professor discriminated between candidates and if all the interviews were conducted with the same vagueness.

In the second interview, Monica indicates that she was best able to formulate ideas about the poem through prompted discussion. However, it is a good idea to try and come up with a couple of interesting ideas on your own to give the impression that you are an original thinker.

On the whole, Monica never felt at any phase that the interviewers were trying to intimidate her; she sensed that their overriding concern was to test her capabilities.

The best attitude to have when going for an interview is that it will be a good experience, and that it is possible to enjoy it. After all, there are few occasions where someone so expert in their field, and the field that you wish to enter, devotes such close, personal attention to you.

Monica found that the most exciting part of the whole experience was the fact that it was so personal and no one who has taught you or who knows you will ever know what you said!

8

FURTHER INFORMATION

OXFORD CONTACT DETAILS

Oxford Colleges Admissions Office
University Offices
Wellington Square
Oxford OX1 2JD
Tel: 01865 270207
www.ox.ac.uk

Disability Adviser
University Offices
Wellington Square
Oxford OX1 2JD
Tel: 01865 280660
www. admin.ox.ac.uk/access

For alternative prospectuses:
Oxford University Students' Union
Thomas Hull House
New Inn Hall Street
Oxford OX1 2DH
Tel: 01865 270777
enquiries@ousu.ox.ac.uk
www.ousu.org

CAMBRIDGE
CONTACT
DETAILS

Cambridge Admissions Office
Fitzwilliam House
32 Trumpington Street
Cambridge CB2 1QY
Tel: 01223 333308
admissions@cam.ac.uk
www.cam.ac.uk

Cambridge University Students' Union
11–12 Trumpington Street
Cambridge CB2 1QA
Tel: 01223 356454
www.cusu.cam.ac.uk

University Disability Advisers
Disability Resource Centre
Keynes House
Trumpington Street
Cambridge CB2 1QA
Tel: 01223 332301
Textphone: 01223 766840
ucam-disability@lists.cam.ac.uk

Widening Participation at Cambridge and GEEMA
    (Group to Encourage Ethnic Minority Applications)
Tel: 01223 742170
access@cao.cam.ac.uk

For STEPs:
STEP Office
OCR
1 Hills Road
Cambridge CB1 2EU
Tel: 01223 553311

OTHER CONTACT DETAILS

MPW
90–92 Queen's Gate
London SW7 5AB
Tel: 020 7835 1355
www.mpw.co.uk
london@mpw.co.uk

UCAS
Rosehill
New Barn Lane
Gloucestershire GL52 3LA
Tel: 01242 227788
www.ucas.com

MAP OF THE OXFORD COLLEGES

MAP OF THE CAMBRIDGE COLLEGES

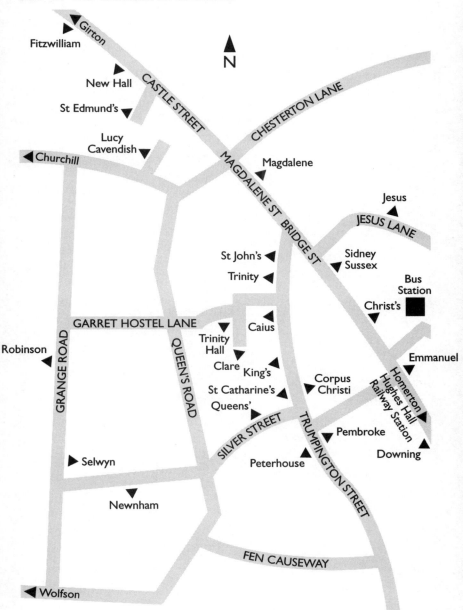